CALLED

CALLED

New Thinking on Christian Vocation

M. BASIL PENNINGTON, O.C.S.O.

The Seabury Press / New York

1983
The Seabury Press
815 Second Avenue
New York, N.Y. 10017

Printed in the United States of America

Library of Congress Cataloging in Publication Data

Pennington, M. Basil.
    Called, new thinking on Christian vocation.

    1. Vocation, Ecclesiastical. I. Title.
BX2380.P4 1983   248.4'8203   83–652
ISBN 0-8164-2472-1

To
SISTER GABRIELLE JEAN
and
all those whom we have had the privilege
of serving
in vocation ministry

Contents

Foreword

Some people write books because they like to write. While writing can be hard work, it is yet an enjoyable creative experience. Other people write because they have something they want to say, there is something in them that needs to be expressed. But there are other reasons, too. I write because I love and I want to share what I have received. *Freely have you received, freely give.*

As I sit down to write, then, I have to ask myself: with whom do I want to share what I have received?

Over the past four years I have had the privilege and joy of serving my community as the vocation father. (I do not like the term director. I believe only One can truly direct the human person: the Spirit of God. Saint Paul assures us: *Eye has not seen, nor ear heard, nor has it entered into the heart of the human person what God has prepared for those who love him, but the Holy Spirit makes it known to us.*) In these years of service, I have learned a good bit more about the way God works with us, giving direction to our lives, drawing us to himself by a calling that we speak of as vocation. It has been a time of growing insight for me, especially through the open sharing of the thousand and more persons who have allowed me to listen with them as they sought to discern the precise nature of their divine call.

We are called, we are constantly called. The whole of Christian life is an answer to a call—a call that is expressed in creation, re-creation, and the intimate urgings of love. But there are moments in the journey of response, when we are called upon to make a decisive response that will have a major effect on our journey and largely determine the context within which we will make our daily response. As we move toward such momentous decision, we can experience a very trying time, especially if we do not have the good fortune of having a spiritual father or mother or a friend walking with us, helping us to listen and discern. So, in this book I want first and foremost to reach out to those of you who are at such a point in your journey in the hope of providing some support and encouragement. The insights I have received and can share may be of some help. At least, may my sharing say: I am with you. You are not alone. Your struggle toward decision is a common human experience.

I think, too, of those of you who are in vocational ministry, and I want to reach out to you. Sometimes your precise role among the people of God and the true nature of your ministry is misunderstood. False expectations are placed upon you. You sometimes find yourself in an isolated position. Your lot is not always the happy one it should be. I want to reach out to you and share some of the joy I have found in vocational ministry. It might, also, be of some value to those of you who are seeking help from a vocational minister to see something of the relationship from his or her side.

For some of us, vocation ministry is our present vocation. For a period of our journey, whether as a layperson, priest, or religious, we have been called to serve others in a ministry of discernment. For many others, vocational ministry finds its place within another vocation. Everyone in ecclesial ministry will at times be asked to help in this area. And this is probably equally true of those of you in education and those in general counseling. May these pages be of some help and inspiration to each one of you.

As I write this, I think also of parents. Vocation touches your lives in many ways. You have your own vocation in married life and parenthood—or in single life and parenthood. As parents, you are called to exercise a certain vocational ministry in regard to your offspring. And as loving parents, in a special way, you share in the vocational search of your children. Your ability to understand and walk with your daughters and sons during their most difficult search can be immensely significant and supportive.

In the end, I write for all. For the vocation of each one of us and our response to it is necessarily in the context of the whole Christian community, the whole human family. How we lead our own lives affects every other woman, man, and child on the journey with us, as well as those who will follow after. God does have a plan. If we fully participate in it according to the gifts he has given us, and in the full exercise of our freedom, which is love, our lives will profoundly affect the lives of everyone else.

A question that confronts an author today is how to handle the masculine/feminine, since the American language does not yet possess an *uter* ("both"—in contradistinction to neuter, "neither"—sex) vocabulary. I might be justified here in using the masculine as almost all my experience in vocation ministry has been with men, and, of myself, I would be slow to apply this experience and what I have learned from it to women. However, in my sharings with vocation ministers, I have been assured repeatedly by women in vocational service who work mostly with women that what I have to share applies for the most part equally well to women. So I do want to address myself to both women and men and speak of both. I will fall back on the statement found in the Code of Canon Law: What is said here even if expressed in the masculine applies equally to women unless by the nature of the case or the context it is evident that this is not so. And I ask the kind indulgence of all for this. I know this way of handling things leaves me feeling uncomfortable but a constant recourse to s/he, wo/men, him/herself and the like makes for awkward reading. May she or he be blessed who helps us to come up with a satisfactory "uter" or inclusive vocabulary.

This volume is by no means meant to offer a magisterial study of Christian vocation. I hope, though, that what I do say will not be lacking in depth. Indeed, I will be treating of the deepest of realities, of God himself and our relation with him and each other, but not in a theoretical way, by way of theological reflection. Rather my approach is quite personal, practical, and pastoral. I intend to write of theological realities but only to the extent that I have made them my own, that they are part of my own lived experience as a vocation father. I do believe that life should be grounded on a solid theology, an understanding of what has been offered to us through the precious gift of Revelation. It is the Revelation that lets us know who we really are and to what we are called. Without it we are far from knowing what our lives are all about.

As I have already mentioned, all that I share here has already been shared, and more than once, with men and women actively engaged in vocation ministry, as well as many others. My thought has been greatly enriched in the course of such sharing and I am grateful for the contribution each has made through his or her sharing, questions, feedback, and reflections. I am grateful, too, to the many candidates who have given me so much as I sought to serve them. I am grateful to my abbot and community for the opportunity so to serve and for the opportunity now to share what I have received. Finally, I want to express my gratitude for the patient and loving labor of a sister who turned my scratch into a legible manuscript. As I thank God, the source of all this goodness, I ask him to bless each of these benefactors and each of my readers so that all of us working together under his love and grace can make a real contribution to the building up of the Body of Christ and its redeeming mission in a very needy world.

Fr. M. Basil
Monk of Spencer

CALLED

1

Called

Are you called?

Yes. Emphatically! Whether you are a priest or a minister, a religious or a married person, a single or someone in partnership—you are called. And this is true even if you were not a Christian. Your very being is a call. And infinite love calls you forth from nothingness into actuality, into being, into life, into love.

In the beginning was the Word. God said *"Let us make man in our own image, in the likeness of ourselves"* . . . *male and female he created them.* God spoke a word and we were called into being. God, the immutable, is ever speaking his word and we are at each moment summoned to be: We are, in the most fundamental way conceivable, called—called into being. Our very being, all that we are, is a response to his basic call to us to share his being, his goodness, his beauty, his life. *Through him all things came to be, not one thing has its being but through him. All that came to be has life in him.*

And he made us with minds to know and hearts to love. Minds with an insatiable desire to know, to know all truth—a desire that can be fulfilled only in knowing him. And hearts with an insatiable desire to love, to love an infinite, unlimited good—a desire to love that can be fulfilled only

1

in loving him. We are called to know and love God by the very makeup of our being, by the potency that we *are*.

All creation is made for the glory of God. All that is made participates in the goodness and beauty of God and is meant to proclaim that goodness and beauty, and return it to him in acknowledgment and praise. But it is only when it is perceived by the human mind and referred back to God freely through the human heart in acknowledgment and praise that it does most properly and worthily fulfill its purpose. The human person, by his very nature and his relation to the rest of creation, is called to be the high priest of creation. In him everything's goodness and beauty are raised to the level where they can consciously and freely bespeak God's glory. To this priesthood we are all called— to mediate the glorification of God by all creation, raising it to a new level by our understanding and acknowledgment. *Ever since God created the world his everlasting power and divinity—however invisible—have been there for the mind to see in the things he has made.*

This is a sublime vocation.

But something even more wonderful has happened to us. We have been baptized into Christ. We have been made one with the very Son of God, in a oneness that is beyond anything we can possibly conceive. *I live, now not I, but Christ lives in me.* We are called, called again, called into sonship. *You are my son, this day I have begotten you.* We are called like the Son ever to be to the Father in that Love, who is the Holy Spirit. This is one basic Christian vocation, common to us all and giving meaning to all else that we do. It is a sublime vocation. It summons us into the inner life of the Trinity.

We move along in the march of time, always searching, always hoping, always on the move toward fulfillment and completion. Not so with God. He is ever complete in the completeness of the eternal "now." And in him we are complete. By faith we can step out of the framework of our created time into his eternal "now" and be at rest in completeness. This is the grace of contemplation, a grace offered to every faithful Christian. God's call to friendship and intimacy is not the prerogative of a few. It is the common call of all Christians shared in part with our Jewish brothers and sisters—all the sons and daughters of the Book.

Many centuries ago God called Abram out of Ur of the Chaldeans, he called him to friendship in such a way that he gave him a new name, Abraham, dined in his tent, and even allowed him to bargain with him. It was the first step toward mending a broken friendship. For in God's original plan Adam was to be a friend. They walked together in the cool of the evening among the trees of the Garden of Eden. Yes, this may be a "myth" but it expresses a reality, a theological reality. God made man to be his friend. And more than a friend, if that can be said: an intimate, a lover, a sharer of his very life and being. Through the Prophets he again and again used the image of the lover, the husband who in a folly of love pursues a faithless wife.

As God called forth man and woman, he called them, too, to intimacy with himself. And he will not be put off by a "no." He called Abraham and Sarah, Isaac and Rebecca. He repeatedly called their descendants. He called Moses and Aaron to sanctify them. He called Deborah to judge them, David to shepherd them, and Solomon to lead them wisely. And each in turn failed. In the end, *I will send my son. Surely they will respect him.* And that Son wept: *Jerusalem, Jerusalem. How often I would gather you as would a mother hen gather her chicks beneath her wings, but you would not.*

Many are called, he said, *but few are chosen.* In his design, of course, all are called. He died for all. But he has given to his members the responsibility of delivering that call. *Go forth and teach all nations.* If not all have heard that personal call—*I call you no longer servants but friends, because I make known to you all the Father has made known to me*—it is because we who have heard the call have not heeded. *Freely have you received, freely give.* We have, all too many of us, failed to pass on the call, and failed to live our response in such a way that our lived witness would proclaim the call of his love.

Few are chosen because few choose. *Behold, I stand at the door and knock. If one opens, I will come in and sit down side by side with him and sup with him.* The Lord made us. He knows us. And he respects us, more fully than anyone else. He knows that the greatest thing he has given us is our freedom, our power to love. He will never violate that freedom. He will never force himself on us. *Behold, I stand at the door and knock. If one opens* . . . Artists have depicted the scene with our Lord knocking on a door which does not have any handle on the outside. It can be opened only from within. He knocks. It is his persistent call. He wants to come into our lives, our hearts. He wants to be our intimate friend.

The Second Vatican Council spoke of this as the universal call to holiness. In speaking of the Church it spoke of this first before it spoke of the more particular calls to religious life or to ministries among God's people. Let us listen to the Holy Spirit speaking through the Council Fathers:

All in the Church, whether they belong to the hierarchy or are cared for by it, are called to holiness, according to the Apostle's saying: *For this is the will of God, your sanctification.* . . . It is expressed in many ways by each individual who, in his own state of life, tends to the perfection of love . . .

The Lord Jesus, divine teacher and model of all perfection, preached holiness of life (of which he is the author and maker) for each and every one of his disciples without distinction: *You, therefore, must be perfect, as your heavenly Father is perfect.* For he sent the Holy Spirit to all to move them interiorly to love God with their whole heart, with their whole soul, with their whole understanding, and with their whole strength, and to love one another as Christ loved them. The followers of Christ, called by God not in view of their works but by his design and grace and justified in the Lord Jesus, have been made children of God in the baptism of faith and partakers of the divine nature, and so are truly sanctified. They must, therefore, hold on to and perfect in their lives that sanctification which they have received from God. They are told by the apostle to live *as is fitting among saints and to put on as God's chosen ones, holy and beloved, compassion, kindness, lowliness, meekness, and patience,* to have the fruits of the Spirit for their sanctification.

It is therefore quite clear that all Christians in any state or walk of life are called to the fullness of Christian life and to the perfection of love; by their holiness a more human manner of life is fostered also in earthly society.

The forms and tasks of life are many but holiness is one—that sanctity which is cultivated by all who act under God's Spirit and, obeying the Father's voice and adoring God the Father in spirit and in truth, follow Christ, poor, humble and cross-bearing that they may deserve to be partakers of his glory. Each one, however, according to his own gifts and duties must steadfastly advance along the way of living faith which arouses hope and works through love.

We are all called. It is a gentle call. *God was not in the earthquake . . . nor in the fire . . . nor in the mighty wind,* but in the sound of a gentle breeze. It is an insistent call, a persistent call. He never gives up and goes away. *Behold I stand all the day long.* But it is a respectful call. We might say a humble call. (How awesome is the humility of our God!) A call in no way merited; a call almost too good to be true; yet, nonetheless, a true call to intimacy with God himself.

This is the fundamental call, the common call of all Christians. All other calls are in reference to it, particular ways in which to respond to it. But, alas, *the fascination of trifles obscures the good. Few are chosen* because few choose to hear the call and heed it. But even among those who do hear, the call is often muffled. We are too busy listening to other things. And even when we do turn to listen, we have allowed so much of the cacophony of a disordered response to creation into our hearts that the din is almost insurmountable. We need to incorporate into our lives the ancient Christian practice of *lectio divina.* Although the words would be literally translated "divine reading," they might be more aptly expressed as listening to the Divine. (It does come from a period when relatively few could read—it was a question of listening to another read, or listening to one's own memory play back what had been heard.) It is a question of taking some time each day, stepping aside for a few minutes—ten or fifteen would be good—and letting the Lord speak to us through his revealed word. *I call you friends, because I make known to you all that the Father makes known to me*—the inner life of the Trinity. It is only a friend who shares his most intimate experiences, the plans and hopes that flow from his shared love. The Lord wants to tell us about himself, his love for us, his plans for us. *No one knows the Father but the Son, and no one knows the Son but the Father and those to whom he wills to reveal him. Greater love than this no one hath than that he lay down his life for his friend. That they may be one, as you, Father, and I are one, that they may be one in us.*

Each day we need to take some time to listen, to break through the obscuring din of trifles, to hear the Word of God, the message of love and friendship. And then we need to keep it, to make it our own, let it form us, 'til it calls forth a response—prayer—'til it calls forth our whole being—contemplation. *Be still and know that I am God.* It is to this that we are fundamentally called, to this intimacy with God, that embrace of love that generates life, that transforms us, renews in us Adam's lost likeness, that makes us one with God.

Unless we have first grasped this, there is really no sense of speaking of vocation in a Christian context. Christian marriage cannot be properly understood apart from this, and the vocation is to *Christian* marriage. Call to partnership in Christ, to Christian community, to ministry among God's people, only has its true and full meaning in this context. Realize your call to intimacy with God, to union with him in the embrace of contemplative love—then you can properly raise the question as to other more particular callings within this call and in service of this call. This is Christian vocation: a call to be with Christ in a particular way among his pilgrim people, but always as one of the pilgrims journeying with all the others toward the unending marriage feast—our marriage feast. And already on the journey we are called to a lover's intimacy. All other love, all other intimacy for the Christian is a reflection of this, a sacrament of it, a participation in it. *The first command is to love the Lord your God with your whole mind, your whole heart, your whole soul, and with all your strength; and the second is like unto this. . . . I give you a new command: you are to love as I have loved.* The exigency of our being is so great that it is spoken of as a command. Yet love ever remains free. It is a call, a call to each one of us to awesome intimacy.

We are all called!

2

A Theology Of Vocation

The word "theology" comes from two Greek words: *theos* and *logos*, literally, a word or discourse *(logos)* about God *(theos)*. The classical Western definition is *fides quaerens intellectum*: faith seeking understanding. The human mind applies itself diligently and persistently to the data of faith, seeking to understand it more fully by reflection, analysis, and synthesis. The great medieval *summae* sought to gather all of theology, an analytic synthesis of the whole of the revelation, into one coherent ordering.

A voice from the earlier monastic tradition speaks a little differently: "The theologian is the one who prays. If you truly pray you are a theologian." We immediately notice that the father of the desert, Evagrius Ponticus, does not speak of an abstract science of theology, but of the concrete person, the theologian. Theology is not primarily something to be written out in books but is a living reality in the human mind and heart. The heart is especially to be emphasized. For theology is the science of God, knowledge and understanding of God. And God, like any person, is really known only by the one who loves him. Love knowledge, as Saint Thomas Aquinas and William of Saint

9

Thierry—both echoing the tradition and our own personal experience—tell us, goes far beyond the reaches of the analyzing intellect.

The patristic approach also underlines another reality: the real presence of God in all and everything. We cannot think about or examine God or the things of God as if he were not personally and dynamically present. It is he who personally makes these facts present to us here and now and, from within, enlivens us to respond to them. All is from him, both objectively and subjectively. Under the impulse of his grace we respond to his Revelation. It should be a response not to his Revelation as something apart from him, but to him in his Revelation now presenting himself to us in that Revelation. In other words, prayer. The theologian, in the truest sense—the one who responds to the Revelation and studies it as it truly is—is the one who prays.

Let us take a few minutes, then, to be theologians in this sense and prayerfully consider some of the data of Revelation which speak of call.

As I have already mentioned, our essential and basic call comes in creation itself: *God said "Let us make man in our own image, in the likeness of ourselves."* The Fathers have pointed out that we were originally made in both the image and the likeness of God. The image involves our essential nature, which gives us the capacity to be elevated to know and love God; the likeness is a thing of grace, a participation in the divine nature, by which we actually do know and love God, as he knows and loves himself, as a friend. The image cannot be lost as long as we exist. The likeness can be. This call to friendship and intimacy, expressed by God in the very creative act—the human race was created in grace—was rejected by the father of our race. This same call is reexpressed to each one of us in Christ in our baptism, which is both an expression of the call, a re-creation, and a response to it on our parts as we accept baptism. All the rest of our Christian life is a living-out of the response. All other calls to us are calls to live out this call in particular ways.

Adam said "no" to the initial call to the human family to live in grace and friendship with God. His descendants reechoed this "no" again and again in many ways. But an inexhaustible love will not be put off. God called and called and calls again.

> Then God said to Noah, "Come out of the ark, you yourself, your wife, your sons, and your sons' wives with you."

The human family is called forth out of the destructive flood of sin. Sin is washed away. A renewed life is expressed. We can begin again as a race called to divine friendship.

> Yahweh said to Abram, "Leave your country, your family and your father's house, for the land I will show you. I will make you a great nation; I will bless you and make your name so famous it will be used as a blessing."

God's calling goes on. He reaches out to particular individuals, but in the service of a people, and ultimately all people. God called Abraham to be in some way a friend. He visited him repeatedly and spoke with him: *Shall I conceal from Abraham what I am going to do?* And he called him to be the father of his people.

God reached out to a sinful race which was suffering for its sin and step by step prepared the way for not only liberation but a renewed call to intimacy. It was a long slow process where first an awesome God evoked a fearful and hopeful response that enabled his people to break away from their fleshpots.

God called to him from the middle of the bush. "Moses, Moses!" he said. "Come no nearer. Take off your shoes, for the place on which you stand is holy ground. I am the God of your father, the God of Abraham, the God of Isaac, and the God of Jacob." At this Moses covered his face, afraid to look at God.

Ordinarily when we first perceive God in a personal way calling us in faith, we are convicted of our own sinfulness and uncleanness, our unworthiness to approach, to be close, to have communication with the All Holy. The initial experience of God's call usually creates within us a fear. We say with Isaiah:

What a wretched state I am in! I am lost, for I am a man of unclean lips and I live among a people of unclean lips, and my eyes have looked at the King, Yahweh Sabaoth.

But God, one way or another, reaches out to us, to heal this, to prepare and renew us for the mission and ultimately the intimacy he wants for us.

Then one of the seraphs flew to me (Isaiah) holding in his hand a live coal which he had taken from the altar with a pair of tongs. With this he touched my mouth and said: "See now, this has touched your lips, your sin is taken away, your iniquity is purged."

We have then the courage to hear and respond to the call:

Then I heard the voice of the Lord saying: "Whom shall I send? Who will be our messenger?" I answered, "Here I am, send me."

If we are tempted to say with Jeremiah: *Oh, Lord Yahweh; look, I do not know how to speak: I am a child*, yet we begin to realize the truth of the words of Yahweh:

> Before I formed you in the womb I knew you, before you
> came to birth I consecrated you; I have appointed you
> as . . . .

Divine predilection is evident in the Old Covenant and
in the New. Years before God called out from the sanc-
tuary: "Samuel, Samuel," he spoke through the heart of
the Prophet's mother, Hannah: *I will give him to Yahweh
for the whole of his life and no razor shall ever touch his
head*; and he confirmed it in the prayer of his priest, Eli:
May the God of Israel grant what you have asked of him. As
the fullness of time approached, God's action was more
immediate and clearer:

> Then there appeared to him (Zachariah) the angel of the
> Lord, standing on the right of the altar of incense. The
> sight disturbed Zachariah and he was overcome with
> fear. But the angel said to him, "Zachariah, do not be
> afraid, your prayer has been heard. Your wife, Eliza
> beth, is to bear you a son and you must name him John.
> He will be your joy and delight and many will rejoice at
> his birth for he will bring back many of the sons of Israel
> to the Lord their God. With the spirit and power of
> Elijah, he will go before him to turn the hearts of fathers
> toward their children and the disobedient back to the
> wisdom that the virtuous have, preparing for the Lord
> a people fit for him."

If old Zachariah had his doubts hearing a prophetic word,
even in hearing the very call, we too can have difficulty in
discerning the Lord's voice.

> Once again Yahweh called, "Samuel! Samuel!" Samuel
> got up and went to Eli and said, "Here I am since you
> called me." He replied, "I did not call you, my son; go
> back and lie down." Samuel had as yet no knowledge of
> Yahweh and the word of Yahweh had not yet been

revealed to him. Once again Yahweh called, the third time. He got up and went to Eli and said, "Here I am, since you called me." Eli then understood that it was Yahweh who was calling the boy and he said to Samuel, "Go and lie down, and if someone calls say, 'Speak, Yahweh, your servant is listening.'" So Samuel went and lay down in his place. Yahweh then came and stood by, calling as he had done before. . . .

From this passage we learn a number of things. If we are rightly disposed, like Samuel, to respond to all legitimate calls from the Lord, whether they come directly or indirectly, even if we repeatedly seem to make mistakes or actually do make them in the process of discernment and turn even repeatedly in the wrong directions, an untiring God will keep calling until we find our way. God called Samuel four times! This passage also highlights the importance of the role of the spiritual father. Even such an obtuse and poor man of God as the priest Eli was in the end, by God's grace given in response to the humble faith of his disciple, able to help Samuel to discern and respond to his call. He gave Samuel the necessary direction so that Samuel was able to respond to God.

The calls we find in the Bible include two dimensions: First, there is the call to the individual which is meant to lead to a growing personal union with God. Abram became Abraham from whom God could not conceal secrets, *whom God will love forever. He was called the friend of God.* Moses, if at first awed and stripped before God, was led up into the cloud and was allowed to see the very glory of God even if only in passing. *Yahweh would speak with Moses face to face, as a man speaks with his friend.* Again and again God defended him against the jealousy of the others, and eventually took him mysteriously to himself. David, despite his repeated sins, was God's beloved and *Yahweh his God was with him.* In the fullness of time God-become-man would speak to us all as friends: *To you my friends, I say . . . I shall not call you servants any more, because a servant does not know his master's business; I call you friends, because I have made known to you everything I have learned from my Father.*

At the same time, the call to friendship, to intimacy, is also a call to be one with God in the work of salvation, to be with him in bringing his people to fullness. Abraham was to father them, Moses to liberate them, David to shepherd them, the disciples of Jesus *to fill up what is wanting in the passion of Christ* for the redemption and glorification of all. We are called to serve. *No servant is greater than his master, no messenger is greater than the man who sent him.* The Son of man came *not to be ministered unto but to minister.* We are called to serve. Yet God does not merely use us as servants, as instruments. In the serving we find our own glorification. Christ descended *for us and for our salvation.* For us he died and rose and ascended. Yet no one received as much glory from his mission as did he himself. We are called to serve that we might be glorified. It is because we are friends that God wants us to be partakers in his salvific mission and glorification. *Father, I want those you have given me to be with me where I am, so that they may always see the glory you have given me.*

Another aspect of vocation, of being called, that is very clear from the Scriptures is our freedom to say "no." Adam and Eve said "no" to the exigencies of divine friendship. Repeatedly their descendants were slow or remiss in their response:

> I hear my Beloved knocking.
> "Open to me, my sister, my love,
> My dove, my perfect one,
> For my head is covered with dew,

My locks with the drops of night."
—"I have taken off my tunic,
Am I to put it on again?
I have washed my feet,
Am I to dirty them again?"

When Israel was a child I loved him, and I called my son
out of Egypt. But the more I called to them, the further
they went from me . . .

The Son of God filled with maternal compassion would
lament: *How often have I longed to gather your children,
as a hen gathers her brood under her wings, and you
refused.*

God calls and we are free, free to follow:

"Come and see" Jesus replied; and so they (John and
Andrew) went. . . .

My Beloved thrust his hand
through the opening in the door;
I trembled to the core of my being.
Then I rose
to open to my Beloved . . .

and free to refuse:

. . . then come, follow me (Christ Jesus). But when the
young man heard these words he went away sad, for he
was a man of great wealth.

There is certainly a sadness in saying "no." There is a
sadness for the one saying "no" to something beautiful.
This is true even when it is to embrace something else even
more beautiful. It is all the more true when it is said in
order to retain something less worthy or the choice of
material goods over a special expression of friendship with

God. It is sad, too, for Jesus who *looked steadily at him and loved him*.

But the Lord, our God, is persistent in his call. Right up to the end, in the very last book of the Revelation, *the Amen, the faithful, the true witness, the ultimate source of God's creation* says: *Look, I am standing at the door, knocking. If one of you hears me calling and opens the door, I will come in to share his meal, side by side with him*, the meal of our love. For he wants to share with us ultimately his very oneness with the Father:

> Those who prove victorious I will allow to share my throne, just as I was victorious myself and took my place with my Father on his throne.

Thus we hear in listening to the Scripture that God does call each and every one by creation and that we remain radically free to refuse or accept his call. Not put off by our refusals, God repeatedly calls us to re-creation. This call of his is always a call to both intimacy and service so that we might the more fully share in his glory.

And thus his call is always present. *If anyone has ears to hear, let him listen to what the Spirit is saying. . . .*

3

In Singleness and Partnership

God calls each one of us personally into being and into sonship. Each of us is absolutely unique. And in that uniqueness we stand absolutely alone. No one else will ever be called just as we. In the end our response to God is alone, in a unique relationship. Each of us is called to his or her own particular friendship with God.

Yet God, as he considered his first human creation, quickly realized (if I may speak so anthropomorphically) that *it is not good for man to be alone.* And he forthwith created for him a helpmate like unto himself. In the ordinary course of things, for most persons their unique response to God's call to intimate love is to be lived out in partnership, supported by that partnership that is a sacrament of God's love for us. Marriage in the Christian dispensation has been elevated or given the deeper meaning of being a symbol and witness to God's love for his Church. Already in the Old Testament, this was evident. God himself, through his prophets, repeatedly used the image of human love and marriage to reveal his ever faithful love for his people. In the New Testament this sacramentality was promulgated and made normative.

One day Jesus was discussing marriage with his disciples. As he told them, man's grossness had led to God's acceptance of a lesser ideal for human marriage. Men were allowed to put their wives aside. But this was not according to God's original plan. And now, since they had the support of the Revelation and the explicit presence of God-in-man and his grace, men and women were called to adhere again to the ideal. Christian marriage, marriage for those who have been identified with Christ through baptism, is to be a sacrament, a sign of his love. And his love is eternal and unfailing. Therefore Christian marriage is indissoluble. As Christ explained this to his disciples, they exclaimed: *If that is how it is between husband and wife, then it is not expedient to marry.* To this Jesus answered: *It is not everyone who can accept what I have said, but only those to whom it is granted.* Christian marriage is a call, a vocation—a special vocation. Christ goes on to speak of celibacy: *There are those who are unmarriageable because that is the way they are from their birth. There are those who have been made unmarriageable by men. And there are those who have made themselves unmarriageable for the sake of the kingdom of heaven. Let anyone accept this who can.* We have always recognized that grace is necessarily involved here. Spiritual insight, vocational grace makes it possible for one to see the choice to be unmarriageable for the kingdom as a good choice, and to effectively make that choice. We have not so readily or clearly seen the importance of vocational grace in the choice of Christian marriage.

I believe we can discern three graces at work in the evolution of a vocation. First there is the grace by which we see the beauty of particular Christian vocations. Man cannot of himself see the beauty or meaning of celibacy for the kingdom, of Christian marriage with its fidelity, of a life of contemplation, and so forth. It is only by God's grace that the transcendent beauty of these particular responses to God's call is perceived. Good Christians, alive in the Lord, cultivating the mind of Christ, do see the beauty of many of the vocations among God's people.

The second grace of vocation is that whereby a Christian perceives one or more of these vocations as beautiful for himself or herself. God is very generous in his endowments. The man who will make a good monk will usually have the gifts to be a good husband and father, to be a parish priest or a missionary. And he may well perceive several of these as good for himself. Or he may not. I think of the happily married men who come regularly to our retreat house. They see the Cistercian life as something very beautiful—but not for them. But many persons today do realistically see several forms of Christian life as very attractive options for themselves.

Finally, there is the third grace, whereby a person chooses a particular vocation and effectively carries through in embracing it and living it with joy and the other fruits of the Spirit. When one is able so to do and live he can be infallibly certain of his vocation, for he cannot do this of himself, only by that grace of God which is vocation.

The ability to perceive and understand Christian marriage—marriage in its fullness as a sign of Christ's love for his Church and his Church's love for him, and therefore as a bond that must be exclusive and enduring—this perception is a thing of grace. The natural person, the ungraced person, cannot perceive this and therefore cannot embrace it. He is not called to Christian marriage. Maybe the call to Christian marriage, especially today, is far rarer than we realize. Or maybe, both in the case of Christian marriage and celibacy for the kindgom, and in the case of more particular calls, the grace is there, but fewer and fewer are heeding it. *Many are called, few are chosen*—because few choose to hear.

Marriage is a sign of God's love, which is precisely the source of its ability to lead to complete self-giving love. Marriage is indissoluble because God is faithful. In the Old Testament God used marriage as a sign. But his people were often unfaithful, so harlotry and betrayal also played their role in the sign. Poor Osee was ordered again and again to accept a harlot wife. But in Christ an unbreakable bond between God and man was forever established. Never would there be any infidelity in him. The Christian is baptized into him. There is no place for infidelity or impermanence in Christian sacramental marriage. Choosing marriage as a Christian is making an eminently Christian decision. It calls for an "I will," a gift of self, that is whole and irrevocable. The couple place their faith in each other, in spite of all the risk that trusting a sinner involves, because they have faith in Christ's power and help.

Some are shocked, we are all pained by the large number of declarations of nullity that are coming out of Catholic diocesan marriage tribunals. The fact is that fewer and fewer of those marrying, especially younger people, have sufficient faith insight, sense of themselves, and estimative judgment to be able to give themselves irrevocably to another. This judgment unfortunately can often be made with some certainty only post factum, and then the attempted marriage has to be declared null. A man cannot give himself to a woman, as Christ gives himself to his Church, if he does not have a good sense of himself as something beautiful that can be given in love. And a woman cannot give herself to her husband, as the Church should lovingly give herself to Christ, if she does not have a sense of herself as someone worth giving in love. Unfortunately all too few today have such a sense of self-worth. The vocational grace that calls one to Christian marriage involves such an insight into one's essential beauty.

For those Christians called to marriage the first call is to

deep union with Christ-God. The call to marriage is a call
to find a helpmate, one who will help the person called to
be faithful and grow in love of Christ. Marital love needs to
be centered in Christ. The human heart wants an infinite
love. If the marriage partners seek this in each other they
are bound to be disappointed and frustrated. The finite of
itself cannot give infinite love. Such false expectation is
perhaps the most fundamental cause for unhappiness, failure, and divorce in marriage. If the married couple are
centered in Christ-God, then their aspiration for infinite
love can be fulfilled and in that love their mutual love can
be limitless.

It is not the place here to write extensively on the vocation to Christian marriage, but I might say a few more
things before moving on. Marriage does involve sex. And
sex is a beautiful thing. Let there be no false prudishness. It
is true that sex has been cheapened and degraded extensively in our present-day world. It has also been made too
much of in a false way. Sex is an immensely beautiful thing.
It is wonderful, full, and fully human. And it is a sacrament
of the divine. When God uses marital imagery to express
his love for his people he is graphically precise. He sees
nothing shameful in the sexual expression of true love.
Awe and reverence perhaps call for reserve. The openness
of the woman to receive her husband bespeaks the openness the Church should have to receive Christ. The powerful, ravishing, fructifying thrusts of her man bespeak the
invasion the Divine wants to make deep into our lives if we
but open ourselves to him. The total coordination of bod-
ies, of vision, breath and breasts, the entwining and rap-
ture as one movement and joy surges through the two tells
of how God wants to be one with us, wants us to be wholly
one with his movement, his will, which is love. In the
fullness of this moment husband and wife are offered the
grace fully to find God, if their lovemaking is a total gift to

each other—for God is such a self-giving love. I know a couple who light a candle before their image of the Sacred Heart when they are going to make love: making love by candlelight, making love in the light of Christ.

Marriage as a Christian sacrament is fully a thing of the flesh. True Christian marriage has a role to reclaim for sexuality the reverence that is due to true beauty and dignity. It is the almost universal degradation of sex that makes it difficult for men and women to perceive Christian marriage as a vocation. In this respect singles in vocation ministry very much need the help of good Christian couples so that those who are trying to discern their vocation can see and identify with—if this is their grace—the vocation to sacramental marriage—a grace that extends to all the interaction, support, and sharing that couples discover for one another over the years.

On the other hand Christian marriage is also a thing of the spirit and of the Spirit. It is a communion of spirit in a love which is the Holy Spirit and flows from the Spirit. Father Patrick Peyton's "The family that prays together, stays together," says more than first meets the ear. It is not just a question of saying prayers together, though this is important. Family rituals of grace at meals, night and morning prayer, and rosary are of inestimable value. But of greater value is spontaneous shared prayer and faith sharing where hearts reveal themselves to each other. Perhaps even more effective, yet even more a thing of faith, is meditating together in a contemplative type of prayer like Centering Prayer. I say this out of the witness of many married couples who have told me that their lovemaking and their whole life communion reached new and unexpected depths of joy and completeness after they began centering together.

Prayer together is important. I think time for prayer apart is also important. Husbands and wives need to give each other solitary time with the Lord so that their mutual love can ever be more centered in him. Thus vocation ministry, which seeks to serve the discernment and fostering of any true Christian vocation, will involve teaching prayer, helping seekers develop the contemplative dimension of their lives so that they can be centered in the Lord. This is equally important for Christian marriage and for Christian celibacy.

Some are called to singleness. Our Lord Jesus was. If the married couple in their total gift of self to each other in love are to be a sign, a sacrament of the love between Christ and the Christian, the single person is called to forgo the sign in order that he might be freer to enter into the reality. As Saint Paul, inspired by the Holy Spirit, wrote to the Corinthians: *An unmarried man can devote himself to the Lord's affairs, all he need concern himself about is pleasing the Lord; . . . I say this only to help you, not to put a halter around your necks, but simply to make sure that everything is as it should be, and that you give your undivided attention to the Lord.* If the celibate forgoes the more obvious sign of love, his embracing celibacy for the kingdom is itself a sign, a mystery, a special call: *Let him take it who can take it.* It is a sign that can so easily be obscured. If the celibate is not a radiant, joyful person, one whose life gives witness to the fruits of the Spirit, that life can easily be taken for, and actually be, one of selfishness and self-centeredness, rather than one centered in God in love. Celibacy should not be seen as only freeing one for service, even though it is of the nature of love for God-Christ that one wants to serve and love all whom Christ loves and serves by his saving life and death, resurrection, and ascension. We must avoid regarding celibacy as primarily ordered toward service. Christian celibacy is first and foremost a call to intimacy with God. If one forgoes that special intimacy with a man or woman that is marriage it is to be freer for a special intimacy with God.

This intimacy, no doubt, like that of man and woman in marriage, is ordered toward fruitfulness—the celibate should be a spiritual father, a spiritual mother—but first of all in both cases the intimacy is the primary thing. Every Christian vocation is a call to intimate love.

Some years ago the Jesuits were planning to move one of their theologates from the wheat fields of St. Mary's, Kansas, to Saint Louis University. They bought a large hotel across from the university campus. At that point they sought advice from the Menninger Institute in Topeka as to how they might best arrange the new facility to promote community life. In a report approved by Dr. Menninger, it was stated that for a person to function well in society as a whole, ordinarily he needs to have in his life one or two intimate friends, a number of good acquaintances, and a large, stable community with which he identifies. The call to celibacy is not necessarily a call to solitariness. In fact, a call to the solitary life is exceptional and relatively rare. There are such calls, and we can hope that the Church will always be blessed with hermits. They are a very clear sign of the all-sufficiency of God. But such a vocation will probably always be rare and most frequently come only after a certain preparation in communal celibate living.

The Christian celibate should prize friendship highly and give himself in friendship. Otherwise, not only will he not develop as a human person, but his choice for celibacy might well be suspect. Rather than being a free commitment in love and communion with the Lord, it might seem a merely human choice not to share life or not to be bothered with others. The unfriendly, unloving celibate is a counterwitness to what is central to Christian life—love.

In this matter of friendship there needs to be a good bit of realism. Friendship cannot be forced. It must be the free response of both persons involved. Yet it does need to be fostered. An openness to receiving the gift of friendship is necessary; a generosity, to give the gift and to respond when it is offered. A fidelity that is demanding is necessary. As Jack Dominion expressed it: "When two people have accepted each other the challenge of love is to maintain the initial splendor of the experience." Intimate friendship implies a choice. We can be intimate with only a few. Time, energy, human resources do not allow for more. Friendship demands time, "wasting time" on our friend.

Celibate friendship also demands a certain caution. As Saint Aelred wrote in his *Mirror of Charity* (his excellent and exciting treatise *On Spiritual Friendship* should always be read in the context of his fuller treatment of love in the *Mirror*), "Friendship is the most dangerous of affections." Its danger arises when freedom of spirit is imperiled by compulsion and attachment. If the Christian who has chosen celibacy for the kingdom does not live a vital prayer life which powerfully centers his love in Christ-God there is danger that intimate friendship with another will become primary and celibacy will be compromised. Yet for all this the good of friendship should not be avoided. Rather its challenge should be embraced. Knowing the emotions and even passion of human friendship can help us to understand better the exigencies and expectations of divine friendship. God is shamelessly passionate in speaking of his desires in our regard. And saintly friends, like Saint Bernard of Clairvaux and Blessed William of Saint Thierry, were passionate in speaking of their friendship centered in the divine passion. Realism is needed here, without losing ideals. Openness with a spiritual father or mother is the greatest help and safeguard.

Initially, singleness is a state of search. It is a time for grounding one's love in God. Then when one discerns his further vocation, it will be chosen as a way of love centered in the Lord, whether it be in singleness or partnership. For some the search goes on and on. If this is due to one's unwillingness or inability to choose, this is not good. Choice is difficult. When I choose to marry one woman I must in some real way give up every other woman in the world. When I choose one particular vocation, I must give up many other very beautiful options. This is not easy, but necessary. It is only through commitment in love that a person ordinarily grows to fullness. But for some persons the search seems long, almost endless. Is there a partner for them in the world? To choose the wrong partner, one who cannot go all the way with us, can be a real disaster, a truncation and frustration. Sometimes the ultimate choice for celibacy comes out of a fruitless search. It is decision by elimination. It can still be in the end a real decision, embraced with freedom and love, and completely fulfilling. For some people that decisiveness never comes. Perhaps we can see such lives as a sign of our deepest, unending search for the fullness of love that is to be ultimately found in the heavenly fruition of God and all in God.

There is a questionable vocation which the Church cannot, in fidelity to her mission, simply ignore or respond to with a generic "no." This is the question of homosexual partnership.

I must confess my own sensitivity to this reality has gone through an evolution. There was a time when I was virtually unaware of the existence of such relationships. And then a period when I shared a common prejudice and closedness toward gay persons. But our Lord has said: *Judge a tree by its fruit.* I have come to know many gay men, some living in long-standing relationships. And many of them are admirable Christians in their love and consideration of their fellow human beings, in their self-giving service, and in their fidelity to their spiritual and sacramental life. God's grace is very evidently working in their lives. This, of course, does not mean that all that they are doing is therefore right. We are all sinners. All the saints, except the Holy Virgin Mary, were sinners. But usually the primary love relation of one's life is a source for all the other loving activity in that life. It is difficult to see how a homosexual couple's central love relation can be essentially vitiated and yet be at the heart of a life filled with Christlike self-giving love. I have more questions than answers.

In her teaching on sexuality the Church is not promulgating positive law of her own creation, like a particular law to attend church on Sunday or fast during Lent. In the matter of sexuality the Church is interpreting natural law, the law that flows from the very nature of things. The Catholic Church has largely drawn her teaching in this area from a static concept of natural law: man has an immutable essence and the law flows unchangingly from this. I would question if this is really an adequate norm for natural law. Man lives in relation with others and with the whole creation. And creation is evolving. I would ask if we do not need a more dynamic concept of natural law. In the beginning man and woman were commanded to increase and multiply and fill the earth. The earth is now quite full (though if man's selfishness would give way to an equitable sharing of the earth and its fullness undoubtedly many more could share its space and resources). There seems to be a widespread and growing conviction that sexual communion can be shared to express and foster the mutual gift of self in love in ways that are not open to the creation of new life. If the evolution of man in his world is at such a point then such expressions of love between those of the same sex might well be seen as legitimate and good in their service of love. This could be so even while granting that the heterosexual expression of love that is open to the fruitfulness of new life has a fullness and completeness that makes it the highest ideal and norm, the more perfect sacrament of divine self-giving, fruitful love. Given the physical makeup of man and woman, a greater connaturality and perfection can be granted in their complementary copulation. But the spiritual union, which is to be expressed and fostered by the physical, is the more important. If a person's true orientation is homosexual, the homosexual union, while perhaps less perfect physically, may yet be the truer sign and cause of love, which is the ultimate norm.

Certainly, it is legitimate for persons to find their most intimate relations with those of their own sex. For those who have chosen celibacy for the kingdom this is quite common, and some would say safer. For those with a homosexual orientation this would be expected. Yet not all homosexuals are called to celibacy for the kingdom: *let him who can take it, take it.* A full physical expression of this friendship might then be expected as a natural supportive expression of the partners' love.

I do not know what response ultimately the Christian community should give to homosexual partnerships. I do believe that the present approach to natural law needs to be profoundly reconsidered in the light of the personalism of Pope John Paul II and the existential conditions of our evolving times. Pastorally, I believe gay persons, who wish to be fully active members of the Christian community while living in partnership, should be received with love and respect and all that this implies. The challenge to assist a gay person who is seeking to discern if he should commit himself to another as his way to grow in love and sacramentalize God's love is something a spiritual father or mother will have increasingly to face. An a priori "no," an imposed call to celibacy, a demand of constant heroic limitation pose serious questions in regard to grace's operation within the reality of creation as it exists. The call to love and to deep union with Christ is certain in regard to all, including those of homosexual orientation. The call to celibate singleness for all gays is not so certain.

Whether one's call to intimate union with God in Christ is to be lived out in singleness or in partnership, each will have his or her role to play in the community. This further concretization of vocation or call we will now consider.

4

Calls Within the Call

God is love. And we are made in the image and likeness of God. Therefore, we are most true to ourselves when we are lovers. We are all called to be lovers—lovers of God and of our fellows, our brothers and sisters, his children, and lovers of his creation, a creation made for us and made for us to love.

God is infinite goodness, beauty, truth, life, and love. God is enough. God alone is sufficient. In himself he can fulfill all our desires, all our potential. Some are graced to see this, to see it clearly and forcefully. *Caritas Christi urget nos. The love of Christ compels us.* So drawn by the love of God in response to his lovableness, we become unmarriageable for the kingdom. We can give ourselves to no other in the marrying way, but must be free to love him.

Others are called no less to union with God but see that the way for them to grow as lovers is through commitment to another human person as a wonderful sacrament of the divine love and lovableness. This is the ultimate question in vocation discernment: in what way can this person best grow in love; what way will best facilitate and support the growth of love in this man or this woman given who they are, their psychological makeup and the graced insight and determination they have. Some need very much the immediate concrete demands and support of a spouse and children to call them forth steadily as lovers. Others will best grow by being free to immerse themselves abundantly in the contemplation of the divine beauty. Still others find their way in a deep union with Christ in his salvific ministry, a celibate bonding that is yet open to incessant demands for self-giving ministerial service.

Love does need to express itself. *He who loves me keeps my commandment. This is my new commandment, that you love one another as I have loved you.* His love was and is total gift. He identifies deeply with us in the giving and the receiving of love. As he depicts the last judgment, it is an examination of service: I was hungry, thirsty, naked, imprisoned, sick, homeless and you responded or failed to respond. In that delightful theatrical presentation of Saint Matthew's Gospel, *Godspell*, one of the condemned pops up and exclaims: "Gee, Lord, if I had known it was you I would have taken you around the corner for a cup of coffee." It is as concrete and simple as that.

Every vocation is a call to grow in love and express it in a particular context. Every vocation is a call to serve in love. This fact gives every work the dignity of a vocation, a call. Each activity we undertake is a response to God's love and presence, a part of his salvific presence and mission.

We are called, even commanded, to pray without ceasing. It is an evangelical precept, repeated by Saint Paul: *Pray constantly.* The first monastic Fathers faced this challenge. How was one to pray constantly and yet accept man's primal penance: *By the sweat of your brow you will earn your bread?* How is one to pray constantly and yet work effectively? Saint Pachomius called for the constant recitation of prayers while working. Whole rituals were established. The bakers had psalms to say while they mixed the dough, other psalms while they kneaded it, and still others while they put it in the oven. And so on. Saint Basil took a more fundamental and intrinsic approach. Stemming from the realization that all that has being is at every moment coming forth from the creative love, the worker realizes the divine presence and activity in the material he is working with, in the tools he is using, and in the energy he is employing. His energy of mind and hand are the divine energy present and operating in and through him. In all that he is doing, man is, whether conscious of it or not, collaborating with the divine in creating and recreating the world and all that is contained therein. If he consciously embraces this reality of collaboration all his labor is prayer. Saint Benedict expressed this concretely when he reminded his disciples that they are to treat the tools they are working with as the vessels of the altar. They are involved in the *opus* of God, the Mass of creation. The integrity of this insight Saint Benedict's biographer, Saint Gregory the Great, expressed graphically when he had the Holy Patriarch of Monte Cassino favored with a vision in which he saw the whole of creation, as it were, under a single ray of light. At every moment all is coming forth from the divine creative Love. In this context it is obvious that all work, all human activity is meant to be participation in the divine. It involves, therefore, a call to collaborate with God. Every human work is a response to a divine initiative. When this response is made consciously, it is prayer and it is fulfilling a vocation, a vocation that is part of Christ-God's salvific mission and recapitulation of the human family as friends of God and stewards of creation.

We must not be too materialistic in our understanding of our role in laboring with God in bringing the creation to fullness. Indeed our more important activity is at the level of love and the spiritual currents of life. Prayer itself and the contemplative dimension of life are most important. God is creatively bringing forth all that is at every moment. He has told us: *Ask and you shall receive.* He has so decided that the way in which he will bring forth the creation in the next moment or on the morrow will be determined in part by what we ask. Prayer is powerful because it harnesses the creative power of God. It is, therefore, not only a very valid way any one of us can express our love and serve others but it is a way in which we all should, and a way in which some who have the insight and the grace can, fully express our love and call.

There is another powerful aspect of the service of prayer, especially when it takes the form of entering into and abiding in a contemplative or meditative state of consciousness.

We had better pause here for a moment to clarify a semantic difficulty. In recent Catholic tradition "meditation" usually refers to a discursive consideration leading to acts of prayer, while contemplation evokes a simple presence to the loved Reality. In current Hindu terminology the two terms have the reverse meaning: contemplation is a more discursive, imaginative consideration and meditation is a simple presence. It is perhaps a sad commentary on Christianity's presence or lack of it in modern Western society when we have to admit that it is the Hindu terminology that prevails even in the West. In what follows I am speaking of the contemplative experience which current parlance refers to as meditation.

There is a bonding within the human species, as in any other. What affects one member, affects the others. Whenever one member rises to an elevated or transformed state of consciousness through meditation or contemplation, in some way the whole human family is lifted up. We have seen this in other species. Teilhard de Chardin has postulated it in the human, underlining the need for the race to rise from the biosphere to the noosphere which he sees ultimately centered in the Omega point, the loving Heart of Christ. Other traditions have spoken of this. Maharishi

Mahesh Yogi has argued that if one percent of the population of any city or area would meditate that locale would be transformed. This is in the end the evangelical teaching of the leaven in the lump; one bit will make the whole rise.

Thus a devoted fidelity to a practice of contemplative meditation can be a most effective loving service, a powerful expression of love. A life dedicated to such practice, a contemplative life which aims at a transformation of consciousness not only for the contemplative but for the whole human family is not only a legitimate vocation, it is a call imperatively needed in our day. Let a simple but alarming fact affirm this: Never in the known history of man has a people or nation stockpiled weapons and in the end not used them. But if we use the weapons we have stockpiled it will be the end of nations and peoples if not the end of the whole race. Never has the human family so urgently needed a transformation of consciousness. Those who devote themselves to contemplative meditation are performing a most basic and loving service. It is a very real response to the call to love and to act.

While some are called to a life wholly geared to contemplation, this contemplative dimension should yet be part of every Christian life. Every response should be sourced in a deep life of prayer, an experiential union with God, so that it will be seen as a true Christian vocation and carried out in view of the completion of the creation and re-creation, the recapitulation of all in Christ to the glory of the Father. Such clarity and understanding will not only have a profound effect on the way the work will be carried out—think of the difference in nursing when the nurse is conscious that the patient is Christ, in waiting on tables when the customer is Christ, in mopping the floor when Christ is going to walk on it—but also it is going to bring a lot of joy into our lives in the realization of the fuller significance of our labor. Fastening bolts on an assembly line can be perceived not as a boring repetitious task but as part of a God-creative process which in the expansion of divine energy and the accompanying love brings the whole toward its redeemed fullness. At first hearing, such an idea, even for one with faith, sounds like a grand bit of high-blown theory. It is only through a contemplative, quiet, open prayer that makes room for the operation in us of those gifts of the Holy Spirit that we received in baptism that we come to realize joyfully that this is reality; our seemingly insignificant humdrum work does have tremendous power and significance. This is why the monk sees his daily manual labor, however menial it may be, not as an interruption in his exalted contemplative mission but as fully a part of it. As so is every labor, great or small, intellectual or menial, honored or despised by this world. The loving Creator acts in them all. *My Father works until now, and I work.* The call to labor with the Creator in human work is a true vocation.

The obvious conclusion to this is that true vocational discernment reaches down into the choice of a profession, trade, or other occupation and even to how we employ what we might call our "free time" or leisure. The Holy Spirit speaking through the Fathers of the Second Vatican Council said:

> All that goes into the makeup of the temporal order: personal and family values, culture, economic interests, the trades and professions, institutions of the political community, international relations, and so on, as well as their gradual development—all these are not merely help to man's last end; they possess a value of their own, placed in them by God, whether considered individually or as parts of the integral temporal structure: "And God saw all that he had made and found it very good" (Gen 1:31). This natural goodness of theirs receives an added dignity from their relation with the human per-

son, for whose use they have been created. And then, too, God has willed to gather together all that was natural, all that was supernatural, into a single whole in Christ, *so that in everything he would have the primacy.* Far from depriving the temporal order of its autonomy, of its specific ends, of its own laws and resources, or its importance for human well-being, this design, on the contrary, increases its energy and excellence, raising it at the same time to the level of man's integral vocation here below.

In the Christian community, and probably more so in the Catholic segment of that, we have tended to relate "vocation" almost exclusively with the call to ministry and/or celibacy for the kingdom. In many instances Christians have not seriously considered marriage as a vocation, have chosen their life's work without consideration of their more fundamental call to follow Christ, have drifted by happenstance into their particular work (a work that might take half their waking hours for forty or more years), and have turned to "extracurricular" activities, interests, hobbies, and avocations merely by attraction or chance, seeing them at times as mere time fillers. Careful discernment processes have usually surrounded admission to the clerical state, carried out, we can hope, in the perspective of the full Christian vocation. But what screening may have been done in regard to other professions has usually wholly neglected such integration.

If I may cite the Second Vatican Council again, the Fathers warned that "one of the gravest errors of our time is the dichotomy between the faith which many profess and the practice of their daily lives"; and it exhorted that there "be no such pernicious opposition between professional and social activity on the one hand and religious life on the other." Rather "let Christians follow the example of Christ who worked as a craftsman; let them be proud of the opportunity to carry out their earthly activity in such a way as to integrate human, domestic, professional, scientific and technical enterprises with religious values, under whose supreme direction all things are ordered to the glory of God." Not only by teaching but by practical and effective vocational programs that are readily available, the Christian churches can foster an integral and fully Christian approach toward vocation. The sense of call is a very beautiful thing for it concretizes God's loving outreach to each individual. The realization that one is called personally by God to fulfill a particular task or role in the overall achievement of his plan of creation puts us in touch with our dignity and the dignity of our task, it gives us joy in a meaning big enough for us. Considering our labor in the perspective of the divine call to love we will evaluate all we do in the light of its potential to help us to grow in Christlike love. Such seriousness, far from undermining the value of leisure and a certain gracious spaciousness, will affirm the importance of such so that life can be truly human, truly divine.

A clear realization of the integrity of Christian vocation postulates that the concerned Christian be effectively committed to the creation of social conditions and working conditions that do allow the space for discernment and the possibility of each person pursuing what is discerned to be his or her true vocation within the society. This will call for educational opportunities and support systems. A young man who is discerned to have a priestly or religious vocation has no difficulty getting the support he needs to pursue it. The Church community readily assists him. But the same is not so true of Christians who discern other vocations even when they are equally intent upon serving the Christian and world community. This inequality calls for some serious consideration as to how we are functioning as a community that is truly inserted in the world albeit on pilgrimage to the kingdom and that fully recognizes and respects the call and mission of each member.

But before we go on to consider inequality in support structures, the Christian community might first have to examine the possibility of certain prejudices existing in her midst that may be impeding some of our fellow Christians from living out their true vocations. At a time when the Catholic community is becoming aware of a growing shortage of priests in the ministry, can we afford not to question the disciplinary decision, albeit founded on some good and even theological values and a tradition of some centuries, which requires that a man who senses a call to ministerial priesthood and wishes to follow it, must also embrace celibacy for the kingdom? Is it right to postulate that a man who senses a call to priesthood *and* marriage must not be allowed to follow his priestly vocation unless he forgoes his call to marriage? Can one successfully embrace celibacy for the kingdom if he is not truly called? Is the violence done by this disciplinary measure not the reason why some, if not many, older priests become bitter, dried up, inhumane, unhappy, alcoholic, self-centered, or hypochondriac? Can this be why there are not more radiant, loving, joyful, life-generating older pastors in our parishes? Is this forced situation not the cause for many defections from priesthood and why not a few priests and seminarians engage in selfish and unhealthy sexuality? Some will say perhaps, that what the Church requires God has to back up if one generously accepts it, but I wonder if that is really good theology? Does it do justice to God, to the responsibility he has given his Church to discern, and to the members of his Church who are sincerely discerning and are confronted by seeming contradiction?

In the same context of the shortage of priests in the Catholic Church we should raise the question—this time, granted, it may be a doctrinal one and that must be discerned by the teaching Church—of a priori and universally denying the call of women to the ministerial priesthood. Does this really ultimately come out of doctrine or prejudice?

Prejudice has, undeniably, its role to play in other cases. We are more ready to acknowledge the evil of prejudice than remedy it in the case of blacks and Hispanics. The possibility of the latter persevering in a Yankee seminary or blacks in a predominantly white seminary, is not great. The whole temper of life and relationships with home and family are different, not to mention language, music, liturgy, diet, general odor, and many other aspects. There has been relatively little done to create Hispanic and black seminaries and religious communities, even while the fewness of vocations to ministry is constantly bewailed. There is less readiness to acknowledge the evil of prejudice against those whose sexual orientation is toward their own sex. The Church offers the anomaly of asserting that celibacy is the only legitimate option for a gay person while excluding him or her from all the institutions established to foster and support a celibate Christian life and to channel celibate energies into ministries of love.

There is then vocation within vocation. In fact, we can say there is vocation within vocation within vocation within vocation. Within the basic Christian call to intimacy with God there is the call to singleness or to partnership. And within this there is the call to service and role. The single person can be called to a life of contemplation, to serve as a doctor, plumber, or factory worker, to be a priest. Again in turn he can be called to exercise this service in the low-income world, the inner city, at the UN, or on a university campus. He may be called to be a priest-teacher or priest-councillor or priest-worker. These latter calls, indeed any of the secondary calls, may be temporary, while still being authentic calls from God. We will look at this question of temporary vocations in our next chapter.

5

Transitions

The soaring divorce rates, the increasing number of singles who shift from one relationship to another, the large fallout from religious and priestly life, the increasing economic chaos—wiping out businesses, closing schools, and terminating other organizations—all underline the fact that a particular call or vocation may indeed not be a "'til death do us part" thing. In time past, stability in vocation was certainly much more common, we might even say it was the rule, with its exceptions as is the case for most rules. But in our time any realistic consideration of call cannot fail to consider the dimension or threat of impermanence that lies within almost every vocation.

This new situation does not arise only from negative factors. Increased longevity has a lot to do with it. It certainly makes fidelity more challenging. More and more couples will be able to celebrate their golden jubilee. Lifetime profession of vows may demand, as in the case of one of our brothers recently buried, eighty years of fidelity. Increased longevity allows ample space for second and third careers. Basic parenting can be completed, leaving a mother with time and energy to go on to other things. (My sister-in-law, mother of five, got her law degree as her youngest went off to high school.) Few persons who have put in their twenty years with the military, the police force, or the fire fighters are ready to call it quits. Even retirement at sixty-five is early for some. I have an uncle who retired from the army in his forties and from the University of Florida at sixty-five, only to go on to start a consulting firm. He recently remarried after more than fifty happy years with his first wife. At this point he gives no signs of retiring as he approaches eighty. We can much more easily continue education while we work—many companies actively encourage this—and thus prepare ourselves to move on to something else. Seminaries for "late" vocations, once almost unknown, are now common and relatively flourishing. Many bishops expect to depend more and more on such vocations in the future. The supports, both moral and practical, for moving on and bettering one's self are many and very real.

All of this is certainly not bad. While it is desirable that teenagers and young adults be urged and assisted to look carefully at their options and make a careful choice of vocation, they will or should grow and develop. It is a part of creative aliveness to be aware of evolving and new potential. There are things we can perceive and do at thirty or forty, no doubt in good part due to the choices made when we were twenty, which we could not have considered then. To close down so that we cannot see this, or even to fear it, certainly does not foster a full aliveness. And, in fact, such an attitude does not foster a positive grounding stability. It rather fosters a stagnation that is apt to lead in the end to instability through disgust. The challenge of new possibilities can call forth a deeper commitment through a growing, constant choice. On the other hand, where we have actually outgrown our first choice (or second or third), expectedly or otherwise, not to look again and move on is paramount to accepting death, at least in part. We can become ossified—skeletons of our potential reality.

The idea of temporary vocations is not as common in our thinking as, perhaps, it should be. In many countries all able-bodied men are expected to put in their time in the military service. For some this will evolve into lifetime careers. The Queen of England's sons are all expected to serve for a time; at present it seems that second son, Andrew, will stay with the military. In some more religious cultures, unfortunately quickly passing from the contemporary scene, all men would don the monastic habit for a shorter or longer period. Among the Hindus, some years (as many as fourteen) as a *bramachari*, a student-monk at the feet of a guru, was the first phase of life. Should we not, perhaps, look at our school years as an integral part of our vocation? Education takes a more and more significant portion of our lives; it is an important part of our lifetime vocation. As regards "temporary monasticism," anyone in vocational counselling will meet men and women for whom a few years in religious life have played an immensely important role in their subsequent vocation. They were as surely called to the monastery for some of their early years as they were called forth to their later role. I think of Mike whose five years with the Alexian Brothers, a nursing order, led to his exceptionally dedicated career as a psychiatric nurse in the U.S. Navy; his service includes a deep theological insight nurtured by prayer as well as an active Eucharistic ministry. Service in the Peace Corps, Vista, and other volunteer groups would be better served if such service were seen as a vocation, albeit temporary.

There are evolving phases in our lives. Our fundamental call to union with God in Christ remains ever intact. I believe it is important to see evolving roles as integrally part of our call. As such, these phases merit due consideration, proportionate to their significance. The choice to embark on a medical career obviously calls for more reflection than volunteering for a year or three years in the Jesuit missions; to get married demands more consideration than making temporary vows. But each undertaking needs to be seriously considered in the light of our basic call; each needs to be seen as part of our response to infinite, eternal love. For this we need grace and the guidance of the Spirit. Life is a whole. And the whole is an exciting, demanding journey into Godlike fullness.

Part of the ministry of the Church should be clear teaching on this matter of the integrality of Christian vocation and an active ministry to assist those who are passing from one temporary phase of vocation to another. As we have said, in our unstable times this involves an ever-growing number of persons. Living through these transitions can oftentimes be far more difficult than making an initial vocational discernment. The need to make such a discernment may come upon us unwanted and thrust itself brutally into our lives. The death or departure of a partner, a limiting accident, a shift in the economic scene, and so many other causes wholly beyond our control can suddenly force us to confront a new, empty life situation, one with a big vocational question mark. The need to shift can come from within; a new realization of who we are and what we really want or need. The process of transition can involve a great deal of loneliness for it can distance us from all that is familiar, from all the bondings of our present, passing, or past vocation. The high costs of transition, emotional and otherwise, can deter us from honestly progressing or lead us to snatch at the first possible solution rather than going through a prayerful discernment process. It is a time when we most need the understanding support of our Christian community with readily available vocational counselling.

There is obviously an unending call to holiness. And there are obviously temporary calls within this call. And there are calls to lifetime commitment. In regard to these latter, a crucial question arises, one very present in our time. Is it possible that the call to marriage "until death do us part" or the call to lifetime commitment through monastic or religious vows is in fact a temporary call?

I am not raising this question in regard to cases when the initial commitment was defective. All too often today the evaluative judgment necessary to make a lifetime commitment is lacking. The realization of this fact is one of the causes for the mounting number of declarations of nullity in the marriage tribunals of the Catholic Church. In such cases, I think, we can hardly speak of a true lifetime commitment. In some cases, even where there is, in the truest and fullest sense, a clear lifetime commitment, the Church recognizes that the mode in which the marriage vocation is lived out can evolve. Married men and women, without terminating their marriage bond, have been allowed to embrace a celibate commitment so long as there is an agreement on both sides, given in one way or another, that they will forgo the exercise of their right to ask for the usual expressions of their marital love. Other traditions recognize such an evolution. Traditionally the Hindu couple, after their children are settled, are free to seek the life of an ascetic or even to withdraw into the forest. I do not think there is any problem in such an evolution, for it is a change of mode and is not contrary to the lifetime commitment.

I raise the question, rather, of the case where the lifetime commitment is abandoned or rejected.

There are a number of training programs being offered today in the United States and other countries. One such program is *est* (Erhard Training Seminar). In *est*, at a pretraining meeting, the rules for the coming sessions are clearly explained and each one who undertakes the training must commit himself to keeping these rules. During training each time a person violates any one of the rules he is challenged: How can you respect yourself if you do not live up to your commitments? It is a good question. And a very accurate one. We cannot respect ourselves if we do not live up to our commitments. Basically then, where we have made commitments we should live up to them. If we have knowingly committed ourselves for life to another person or to a community or to a particular state or service we should be faithful to such a commitment. We owe it to who we are, to the integrity of our person, as well as to the others who are involved. In a very real sense "the others who are involved" is everyone for our integrity or lack of it necessarily affects every other human person. When we are examining our commitments and making our decisions or assisting others in vocational discernment this should be seriously taken into account.

However, we are all sinners. We do fail. I think the Orthodox Churches' policy in regard to marriage is good in this regard. They steadfastly maintain the indissolubility of Christian sacramental marriage. It is a sacrament of Christ's unending fidelity. But they recognize that married persons are sinners. As in all else, so even in their marriage commitment they can fail. Our God is a merciful God. He does forgive the penitent. The prodigal son was restored to his sonship and allowed to try again. The Orthodox Churches, evoking *economia*, the dispensations of Divine mercy, accept the fact that there are failures in marriage, acknowledge the repentance of the sinner, and allow the repenter to try again, in a new union, to grow in love and to show forth Christ's undying love for us. We find a similar *economia*, though perhaps not so clearly explained, in the Western Church's dispensations of monks and other religious who have made lifetime commitments. Perhaps the Churches could learn from each other and extend their application of *economia* to the areas where they have hitherto withheld it.

Failure in commitment may be inherent in an initial

decision and become clear only with subsequent growth. When we make our commitments we may fail to understand and measure ourselves or the vocation properly. Later this becomes evident to us. External authority may not be too ready to recognize such subsequent realization. There can be a conflict here between what we might call the internal and the external forums. I do not think it would be accurate to express this as a conflict between personal and social concerns. That we be responsive to our proper vocations has social implications. If one is compelled to continue in a marriage contrary to his true vocation for the sake of "good" social order the overall effects on the social order will not be good in the long run. When we follow our true vocations we are being socially responsible and fulfilling our proper role for creating and maintaining good social order.

When there has been an error in judgment in making the initial commitment there may well not be any moral failure on the part of the one making the commitment. The frequency of such failure in our day however, should alert vocation counsellors to be sure that they adequately challenge those whom they are counselling to examine themselves and the calling they are considering. Those who are responsible for the good of the social order (that means really all of us, but I am thinking here of those more specifically deputed to this) should be aware of their serious duty to promote adequate vocational counselling by whatever means lie at their disposal.

The possibility of failure is certainly multiplied when two or more persons are involved in the commitment. In a marriage the two spouses may develop in very different ways or at different paces, or an individual may develop more rapidly than his community. This may be due to failure on the part of the other spouse or of the community, but such possibilities should be seen as part of that to which we are committing ourselves. But the person who has, as it were, "grown beyond" his spouse or his community may find that he is in danger of a serious truncation in his further development or even a major threat to his moral well-being. The innocent person or the aware person (rarely in such cases is all the failure on one side only) may see a termination of the commitment as the only way to remain faithful to his primary commitment to grow as a lover of God in Christ. Can such a situation be said to indicate a new call? I would think this might be so, but the discernment should be carefully made. It may rather be a call to continue to embrace a situation that demands a tremendous self-giving love, a special albeit difficult opportunity for growth. On the one hand the commitment was not conditioned on its producing the best or most helpful of situations, even though a partner is supposed to be a helpmate and the community a support. On the other hand I do not think a person should wait until he is in an absolutely impossible situation before discerning a sign that a particular commitment should be terminated. The judgment to be made here is a very delicate one. Separation for a time might ordinarily be the first step in response to a counterproductive situation, especially if the person's physical, mental, or spiritual health is being undermined. In the end, a permanent separation might have to be decided upon so the person can get on with life.

Does voluntary termination of a perduring commitment always imply some failure? In some sense, yes.

In making a lifetime commitment we are making a judgment on ourselves and others (our partner or our community) that they and we have what is necessary for us to find all fullness in and through this relationship to which we commit ourselves. If we do not make such a judgment when making the commitment, this is a failure. If we do make such a judgment and later find it a false judgment, this is a failure, at least in our perception. We may have misjudged because we have evolved in an unforeseen way. Objectively there would be a failure here to foresee the evolution, or at least the possibility of such an unforeseen evolution and to allow for it in the commitment. There may well be no moral failure here. There nevertheless may well be responsibility for failure if we have not evolved as we should have or even deteriorated through our own fault. Each commitment carries with it certain obligations. Committing ourselves to another or to a community does involve taking due care of ourselves, doing what is necessary to continue to grow ourselves and doing what is necessary for the relationship and for the other party or community to grow. Lovers must foster their love-relation, giving it all the time and attention it needs. Celibates for the kingdom must give due time and attention to the king.

Whether there be failure or not, wherever the responsibility might lie, situations can arise where continuing in a life commitment is not productive of a life of love and even militates toward the destruction of such a life. Where such a situation cannot be remedied love calls us to move on— love of God, love of self, love of the other(s)—with a humble repentance for whatever failure may be involved.

With due dispensation where necessary and with consideration of what is due in justice to the community he is leaving, the celibate may move on to another community. Can he also move on to marriage? The celibate should certainly be challenged—is it possible for him to find another situation where he can faithfully and fruitfully continue to live out his commitment?—but the option is open to him. Is the same option open to a married person? Not in the Roman Catholic communion. Perhaps this, too, should be challenged in favor of the *economia* recognized by other Churches. Given a failure in marriage can we be sure that the only God-given vocation a merciful and forgiving Father offers is that of lifetime celibacy? This is a heavy question. Why should a failed commitment to God in celibacy be more readily set aside? Why should a failure to live out a sacrament have lasting consequences for the repenter when failure to live out the reality does not? These also are hard questions. If a divorced person discerns with sureness that he can live a more loving life in partnership—it was the way he was originally called to— even more, if he discerns that he can hope to live a loving life in celibacy only with the greatest of difficulty, a difficulty that may amount to virtually a moral impossibility for him, can a vocation counsellor be certain he is not called to a second marriage?

There are temporary vocations—even where we sometimes do not expect them. This is good. It is good that we are challenged in our vocations—at least at times. Not all the time! We would have no peace and become too introspective. But at times it is good to ask ourselves or face situations that ask us: Is this way I am pursuing, even a profession or a commitment, most life- and love-producing for me? If the answer is "no" we must have the courage to explore and, if need be, to change; or to take what might be the more difficult course and reanimate ourselves to make our commitment once again life-giving. In the case of a lifetime commitment, the challenge is to enter ever more deeply into the mystery of Christ our God's unfailing love. We are called to be perfect as our Heavenly Father. How graphically he depicts himself in Osee's foolish but fruitful love of a harlot. The power of such love to recreate—to recreate a partner, a community, ourselves—should not be minimized. It may well be, in God's design, that this is *the* way to redemption and life for all concerned. Discernment is called for, but the prejudice should be toward fidelity in a redemptive likeness to God our Father.

6

Come and See:
A Vocational Program

Some years ago, during the Second Vatican Council, I had the opportunity to attend at Rome an international conference on vocations. It was sponsored by the Sacred Congregation for Religious and Secular Institutes. One of the things that made the conference especially interesting was the fact that each of us used his own language when he spoke; there was no translation system. On the last evening we had a question box. Archbishop Paul Philippe was drawing the questions from the box. As he drew the last one, he said: "Ah, here is an interesting question: How do you get across to a young person the idea of a contemplative vocation?" A little priest from Brazil, a Salesian by the name of McCale, jumped up to answer. He went a mile a minute in Portuguese; in substance he said: "You bring the person into contact with the life and he intuits the meaning." I found out later that Father McCale had been responsible for many contemplative vocations in South America.

In Jesus' time, as in the fourth century, as in the eleventh century, as in our own century, as in every time, earnest young men have left home and family in search of a master, a teacher who could give them some insight into the deeper meanings of life, who could give them a vision big enough to satisfy the longings that were stirring deep within them and show them a practical way to advance toward such a vision. Young men throughout Judea and Galilee and beyond, and older men and women, too, heard of a *Voice crying in the wilderness* and went forth to ask, *What must we do to be saved? Father, give us a word of life. Are you the One?* John the Baptizer, the first Christian vocation counsellor, made it clear that he was not the One. The Christian counsellor is never the master, the guru. He is always pointing to another, to the Christ. The day came and those gathered around John heard him exclaim: *Look! There! There is the Lamb of God!*

Many listened to John, but only two really heard him, John and Andrew. They immediately followed after Jesus. Jesus turned to them and asked them what he asks all of us: *What do you want?* The God who made us, respects us as no one else does. He reverences his creation because he knows its beauty and worth, it being a loving participation of his own beauty and worth. He knows that the greatest thing in creation, the greatest essential quality of man, whom he made in his own image and likeness, is human freedom. This is so because in our freedom resides our power to love. And God is Love. God respects our freedom to choose, and he will give us whatever we choose, whatever we want: *Ask and you shall receive. What do you want?*

John and Andrew knew what they wanted: *Master, where do you dwell?* They wanted to stay with Jesus, with the Master, for being with him, watching him and imitating him, they could hope to come to know the way and to attain the goal. Jesus did have a way for them. He himself is the Way. But they could not understand that yet. If he spoke to them about it, it would not be comprehensible. And so, he responded: *Come and see*. By being in contact with him, in due time they would see, they would intuit, they would know their very special vocation.

Our fundamental Christian vocation is to follow Jesus and come to know that he is the Way, the Truth, our very Life, to be one with him on the way, walking in the truth, living out of his very life in intimate oneness. For each this fundamental call is incarnated in particular calls. It is by coming into contact with Jesus, now living and walking through our lives in other Christians, that we come to perceive the different possible Christian vocations open to us and are attracted to our particular call so that under grace we can effectively choose it. To find our vocation, to understand the grace stirring within us, we have to see Christ, our Way, in a Christ-brother or sister walking in the way we are called. Having heard hundreds of vocation stories, I am convinced that this is the ordinary and most common way if not the absolutely universal way in which Christian vocation is perceived. The Christ-person may not be seen in person but encountered in his writings or through other media. Thomas Merton, through his various works, especially his autobiography, still helps countless men and women to discern their call to the Cistercian life. St. Francis in movies, poetry, and popular imagination puts many in touch with the true grace-inspired aspiration of their lives. *Come and see*. I believe one of the reasons for the recent rapid disintegration of marriage fidelity is that so few per-sons perceive marriage as a true Christian vocation, as a call to sacramentalize Christ's undying love for his Church, because they have not seen intimately enough a true Chris-tian marriage so that they can get in touch with the grace that lies unidentified and frustrated within them. *Come and see*. Every Christian vocation needs modeling, that is a perceptible incarnate presence, so that the person receiving the grace of the call can identify his call and then receive some inspiring assistance in following it.

I would like to describe here a program aimed at fostering discernment of Christian vocations through a "Come and See" approach. This is referred to as "The Cottage Program" because it is centered in a building commonly referred to as "The Cottage." While the program is aimed at assisting any participant to perceive his true Christian vocation—whatever that may be—its location and the actual vocation of the spiritual father directing it especially foster the perception of a particular vocation. I hope, however, in describing this particular program to indicate concrete ways in which similar programs can be set up to foster other Christian calls.

First and above all the program must be supported by prayer. There are particular graces involved in the perception and following of vocation. These graces come in response to prayer. *Ask and you shall receive.* If the Christian community which sponsors a vocation program does not first of all support it by prayer, it may well be wasting its time and other resources in all else it does, condemning all to frustration.

After prayer comes Christian hospitality, a concrete expression of love, joy, peace, kindness, and all the other fruits of the Holy Spirit. There is little hope that anyone will perceive his Christian vocation in an un-Christian expression of the vocation in an individual or a community. Every sincere inquirer should be welcomed, and not only after a grilling, but as soon as his seeking is communicated his sincerity should be acknowledged without undue questioning. This means having a person, a spiritual father or mother, readily available to respond. If a particular Christian vocation is to be especially fostered, this person should incarnate that vocation in an exemplary way. Exemplary does not mean being an undiluted incarnation of the ideal. He should certainly have a clear perception of the ideal, love it, incarnate it in some degree, find joy in it, and at the same time perceive where he falls from it, be reasonably comfortable with this fact, and live peacefully and productively with the healthy tension of lovingly embracing the reality and moving gently but steadily toward the ideal. His incarnation of the ideal, a particular expression of the Christ here and now alive in his Church, enables the seeker to identify the grace he is receiving that calls him to the same ideal. The vocation father's comfortable (in the right sense) acceptance of his own weaknesses and shortcomings and his honest and joyful quest of the ideal in the face of these assures the seeker that he, too, with all his limitations, can hopefully strive toward the same ideal.

The welcome also demands that there be a place for the seeker to *be* welcomed. Hence, The Cottage: a place where room is always available to house the seeker, where he can find space, good space to pray and reflect, to receive instruction and guidance. The Cottage contains five rooms, which can take double occupancy, though single is preferred. Four or five is a good number with which to work. There is a large sitting room well adapted to intimate gatherings around the hearth. The enthroned Bible holds a central place. Along the walls there is a good lending library of books providing information on Christian life, its practices, and its various expressions. In one corner is an alcove where coffee and tea are always available. The attached garage has become a chapel, a quiet refuge for solitary prayer. These facilities and their particular arrangement seem to have proved to be ideal for the program. The vocation father keeps no office in The Cottage but speaks with the men in their rooms—on their turf—or in other informal settings. The Cottage is in the embrace of a larger Christian community and can participate in its Eucharist,

Office, and meals. This is very supportive and seems almost necessary. It certainly is necessary if the program seeks especially to foster vocations to a particular community. If the program is standing on its own it will have to provide these basic needs of Christian community and will, therefore, need more complex facilities.

Granted the provision of these Christian-life basics, the program consists in the integration of four principal elements: sacred reading, contemplative prayer or Christian meditation, a rule of life, and a spiritual father or mother.

Faith comes through hearing. The discernment of a Christian vocation is an act of faith. It calls for a fundamental commitment to God in Christ known through faith. The call, the way to follow Christ and be united to him, can be perceived only in faith. And *faith comes through hearing*: hearing the faith proclaimed in the liturgical assembly, in personal instruction and guidance, in faith-sharing, in the lives of committed fellow Christians. The means though that lies most effectively and constantly open to the average person is sacred reading. We want to foster this in the lives of the persons we are assisting in vocational discernment so that their faith and faith perception will constantly grow. This calls for practical instruction.

We really need to do *three kinds of sacred reading*. Though in practice they can coalesce, and we should always be open to this, it is good to be aware of our various needs and to plan to respond to them.

We need to feed the mind, the intellect, with *sacred study*. Today secular education goes on for many years, through primary and secondary school to college and university for very many. For many persons, however, religious education rarely goes beyond primary school level. *The just person lives by faith*. How is a primary school level of faith education going to be able to give a Christian form and outlook to an advanced secular education? All too often we hear, as I did from a young man recently, that the faith has been left behind. By God's grace it is picked up again but it needs a lot of development if the person is going to become an integral Christian.

The development of doctrine, a deepening of the Church's understanding of the revelation is constantly going on under the movement and inspiration of the Holy Spirit. We had the grace to be living at a time when a most special Holy Father, Pope John XXIII, dared to call upon the heavenly Father in Christ's name and ask for a new Pentecost. And his prayer was heard. This blossomed into an ecumenical council where the fact of the constant development of dogma in the Church, with an ever-increasing understanding of the Revelation through contemplation, meditation, and study, was clearly affirmed. We cannot expect the Holy Spirit to work today through yesterday's theology. We have to keep up to date. Few of us have adequately absorbed the rich teaching of Vatican II not to speak of the significant encyclicals we have received from the recent Popes. Sacred study needs to be part of all our lives.

Then there is what I call *motivational reading*. This is along the lines of what I think is ordinarily meant by spiritual reading. I do not like the term spiritual reading, although it can quite legitimately be used to refer to that reading through which our spirit is fed or, better, through which the Holy Spirit speaks to us. This terminology tends to go hand in hand with the notion of "spiritual life," an expression that I feel undermines true life in the Spirit, something very concrete, real, and in the flesh. "Spiritual" tends to lead to fuzzy thinking and a lack of down-to-earth practicality in the pursuit of our very down-to-earth life in the Holy Spirit.

Motivational reading is reading that is directed more to the will—to move us to respond to reality. We need to motivate ourselves constantly. We are drawn to our particular vocation and all that gives us hope by the vision of an ideal. At the same time, or soon after, we are confronted with the real, in ourselves, in others, in those who reveal the vision to us, in the community we are attracted to join. Three alternatives lie open to us (not counting the option of choosing no alternatives). We can cling to the ideal and reject the real. Those who constantly do this spend life in a fruitless pursuit of something that does not yet exist. We can reject the ideal and settle down in the real. At first this might seem the more "realistic" thing to do, or at least the easiest thing to do. But in the long run it can lead only to frustration, for it is a life that is going nowhere. There is no ideal. Finally, we can keep the ideal, lovingly embrace the real, and constantly seek to bring the real gently toward the ideal. This is the dynamic tension of life, a life full of meaning that is going somewhere.

If we choose the last alternative, and it is the only one that really makes sense, then it is important to keep our vision of the ideal strong and clear so that it can constantly draw us. The real presses in on us from every side. *The fascination of trifles obscures the good.* Daily coping with the real can cause us to lose our ideal or undermine its power to draw us. We need constantly to be renewed in our vision. Motivational reading is one of the means to do this. Our ideal, which is in some way a mystery of faith, is seen more clearly by faith-sharing, by hearing, and we can do this regularly by reading.

There is general motivational reading which reaffirms our fundamental call and the means to respond to it. At times, however, we will become aware of needs in particular areas: the Mass does not call us forth the way it should, the Office is paling, we are struggling with obedience or chastity, and so on. At these times we want help to clarify our vision of the values involved. We can obtain this through sharing with our spiritual father and others. We can also obtain it through motivational reading.

In vocational ministry motivational reading has an important role to play. Through it the beauty of particular vocations are able to reveal themselves to the seeker. All Christian vocational material is based on this. The full significance of the role of motivational reading should guide those who prepare such literature. A Madison Avenue approach will not work. Many religious institutions have not realized this even after unbelievably large outlays of time, energy, and money. The kind of vocational literature that is going to foster true vocations is going to have to operate at the level of Christian faith and help the seeker to identify the movement of grace that is stirring within him. Attention catchers may be all right but more substance that speaks out of the faith experience of the lived charism and communicates is necessary for results. There are many fine books on marriage today, and on priestly, monastic, and religious life—as well as life in particular monasteries and apostolates. In our vocational ministry we can guide people toward the motivational reading that will help them discern and foster the grace they are receiving.

Finally there is *lectio*, or as it is sometimes called, *lectio divina*. This name is usually left in Latin for it connotes a whole process of which sacred reading is the first step. It is geared not so much to the mind or will but to the whole person or to the heart of man, to experience. It begins with receiving the Revelation of God, *lectio*, and letting this Revelation form the heart, *meditatio*, until it calls forth the particular responses of prayer, *oratio*, and blossoms into the total response of contemplation,. *contemplatio*.

We who are privileged to be sons and daughters of the Book can receive the Revelation in an especially full and intimate way: *I no longer call you servants but friends because I make known to you all the the Father has made known to me.* Sitting at our Master's feet and listening to him speak to us through the Book will probably be our ordinary and most fruitful way of receiving the Revelation in ever new fullness. But *lectio* might take the form of recalling what we have heard before, listening to our memories. In earlier times it was more common to commit large sections or even the whole Bible to memory. The Revelation can come to us through the words of a reader, preacher, or faith-full friend. Icons, frescoes, stained-glass windows, art of every kind, and the *opus*, the work of the Greatest of Artists, the whole creation speaks to us if we listen.

If the fundamental Christian vocation lies in intimacy with Christ-God, then a daily encounter with him in his inspired Word, an encounter open to experience of him, is a practice which can have primary importance. As vocation fathers we foster this, giving the seekers a simple concrete method for practicing it. As usual, the method is reduced to the mystical three. First, we come into the presence of God dwelling in the text and call upon the Holy Spirit, who inspired the text and who dwells in us, to make the text speak to us and to help us hear it. This coming into presence might well be expressed physically by kneeling or prostrating, or kissing the text. Secondly, we *listen* to the Lord, speaking to us through the text, for ten or fifteen minutes. I prefer to say listen rather than read to underline the Presence. It is a listening open to response—that spontaneously goes on through *meditatio* to *oratio* and *contemplatio*. If we set ourselves to spend an allotted amount of time in *lectio*, always open to the Spirit to call us further, we are more apt to remain open and listening than if we set ourselves a portion—page, chapter, or paragraph—and experience a push to get the allotment done. Finally, the third point: at the end of our allotted time we thank the Lord, again emphasizing the Presence. It is wonderful that we can get God to sit down with us whenever we want. (would that all his representatives were as accessible!) and take a word.

This is the beginning of the *meditatio*. In earlier times disciples would regularly approach their spiritual fathers and ask for a "word of life." The father would then give the disciple some words of wisdom—often from the Holy Scriptures. In *lectio* the Lord himself gives us a word of life. Some days he very evidently does. Some word of our reading penetrates our being or ignites a light in our mind. One time at Mass we had the gospel reading where Jesus asked his disciples: *Who do men say that I am?* After their assorted answers he asked again: *And you, who do you say that I am?* That word resounded deep within me. I not only made it the point of my homily, I have let it repeat itself again and again within me.

This was the earlier method of *meditatio*. Rather than a lot of thinking and analyzing, making points and using the imagination, the Christian simply allowed a word received from a father or from the Scriptures to repeat itself sometimes on the lips, more often just within, until it formed the heart and called forth the response of prayer, *oratio*, and *contemplatio*.

Some days we read on and on and no word seems to speak to us or stand out in any way. Then at the end of the allotted time we choose a word and carry it with us through the day and night. More often than not, sooner or later, it will burst into fire—it will speak to us or speak to another through us. If each day one word of our Master comes alive in us we will soon have the mind of Christ. Faith grows through this hearing, the faith that helps us discern our true meaning and call in Christ. Daily *lectio* of this sort is one of the important elements in our vocational program.

Lectio naturally, yet supernaturally for it is a gift of grace, leads to *contemplatio*, contemplation. Once we experience this complete being-to God in peaceful presence, we long to return to it and abide in it. Young people especially seek this rather explicitly, though they are more apt to call it meditation. In The Cottage program we try to respond to this desire and facilitate the enjoyment of contemplative prayer by teaching a traditional Christian method to those who do not already have a method. When the men are with us we try to have two or three group meditations (contemplative prayer) a day. This helps them grow in confidence in this form of prayer and prepares them to practice it regularly at home a couple of times a day.

I think this kind of quiet experiential prayer is important. Something happens when the candidate sits in silence with the spiritual father, a rapport builds up, a communication takes place that makes it much easier for them to be one in the discernment process. More important, coming to know himself experientially in the love of God, when he sees himself reflected back to himself in the eyes of God's love, the candidate has a freedom, a sense of self, and a clarity with regard to himself and his giftedness that makes discernment and decision much easier. Certainly, the tensions of the process are dissipated and are replaced with the joy of a loving context.

The traditional method for entering into contemplative prayer that we teach in our program is called Centering Prayer. The name is new but the simple method goes back to some of the earliest Christian sources, to the Fathers of the Desert. I have written extensively of this form of prayer elsewhere so I will give the main points here very briefly. Sitting well supported in a good chair with the back straight and the eyes closed is the best posture for this prayer. After getting settled quietly, we turn in faith to God dwelling in our depths and "be to him" in love. Then, in order to be able to remain completely with him in love and rest with him we employ a love-word (often it is our favorite name for him) which we repeat gently as needed to keep centered on him. We will, almost inevitably, be drawn away from this centering in love by thoughts, sounds, and other pulls. Each time we become aware we have been drawn away we gently return to him by repeating our love-word. Some days we will have to use our love-word almost constantly. No matter; it is the love that matters. We usually propose that this prayer be practiced for twenty minutes twice a day. Shortly after rising and before supper are often good times. *Where the Spirit is, there is freedom.* No hard and fast rules. Only enough structure to support doing what we really want to do. At the end of the prayer time, we let go of the love-word and interiorly pray some more thoughtful prayer, letting the peaceful love flow up and out into life. The *Our Father* is a good prayer here. This method is very simple and allows space for each candidate, however developed he may be, to fill the space with love, opening out into contemplative experience of God. In teaching the prayer, I would recommend it be taught very simply, then be immediately shared, before any further discussion, questioning, or analysis.

The third element of the program is the formulation of a *Rule of Life.* This is a very practical tool not only for helping the seeker to move ahead in the way he wants, but also for providing insight to the spiritual father. Some people react to the idea of a rule; "rule" for them connotes something binding, a cage which will inhibit growth. It should rather be taken as something supporting life, a trellis which allows the climber to reach up toward the sun of justice. Much of the time a vital plant reaches out on its own, away from the trellis. But when it needs help to keep growing in the upward direction it wants to pursue, it has the trellis to lean on for support.

The first step for one engaged in formulating a rule of life is to meditate on the First Letter to the Corinthians, Chapter 2:

> But still we have a wisdom to offer those who have reached maturity: not a philosophy of our age, it is true, still less of the masters of our age, which are coming to their end. The hidden wisdom of God which we teach in our mysteries is the wisdom that God predestined to be for our glory before the ages began. It is a wisdom that none of the masters of this age have ever known, or they would not have crucified the Lord of Glory; we teach what Scripture calls *the things that no eye has seen and no ear has heard, things beyond the mind of man, all that God has prepared for those who love him.*
>
> These are the very things that God has revealed to us through the Spirit, for the Spirit reaches the depths of everything, even the depths of God. After all, the depths of a man can only be known by his own spirit, not by any other man, and in the same way the depths of God can only be known by the Spirit of God. Now instead of the spirit of the world, we have received the Spirit that comes from God, to teach us to understand the gifts that he has given us. Therefore we teach, not in the way in which philosophy is taught, but in the way that the Spirit teaches us; we teach spiritual things spiritually. An unspiritual person is one who does not accept anything of the Spirit of God; he sees it all as nonsense; it is beyond his understanding because it can only be understood by means of the Spirit. A spiritual man, on the other hand, is able to judge the value of everything, and his own value is not to be judged by other men.

We have been baptized into Christ the Son: *I live, now not I, but Christ lives in me.* We have been made most intimately one with the very Son of God, in a very real sense divinized, made partakers of the divine nature and life. In view of this it is clear that, as Saint Paul has said, we cannot of ourselves divine the full meaning of our lives, of that to which we are called. We need to depend deeply on the Holy Spirit who knows the deep things of God to make them known to us. Prayer, therefore, and a great attentiveness to the Spirit is most essential to formulate an adequate rule for ourselves.

We ask the candidate-seeker, after due reflection and prayer, to take four sheets of paper. On the first sheet we ask him to write down as concisely as he can what he wants out of life, what he wants to do with his life—long term and short term. Everyone, of course, wants happiness. But many do not know wherein to find it. Happiness lies in knowing what we want and knowing that we have it or that we are on the way to getting it. Many of us do not know what we want, and this in two ways. On one hand, our very nature as human persons, as Christed persons, has its wants and needs. If we are not in touch with and responding to these needs, there will be a sense of frustration in our lives, perhaps low grade but very persistent, undermining our overall sense of joy and well-being. Within the perimeters of these basic wants and needs there is ample room for the free choice of alternatives. So ample is the choice it paralyzes some. Others are unwilling to choose because every choice means giving up the alternatives to some extent, and they do not want to forgo anything. It is when we *do* give up good alternatives for our choice that we value all the more what we have chosen. In any case, for true happiness, choices have to be made and they have to be realistic. For the man in vocational discernment, the more ultimate concerns might be quite clear. His secondary goal may be precisely to discern what will be his chosen way of life on the way to his ultimate goal.

On the second sheet the candidate will try to list what he needs to do or to have in order to obtain what he wants.

Here he needs to be practical. As a Christed human person he needs sleep, food, friendship, work, study, recreation, exercise, prayer, sacred reading, sacraments, fasting, and so on. He should know how much sleep he needs to function well, and how much prayer and sacred reading to keep alive as a Christed person. He will need to reflect on what he concretely needs to do in his vocational discernment process: look at his different options, consult, possibly use testing, work with a spiritual father, and so forth.

Next, the seeker is asked to look back over the last six months or whatever might be a significant period and ask himself: What has been preventing me from doing what I want to do, getting what I want to get out of life—in myself, in others, in my life situation? These things he lists on the third sheet.

The fourth sheet is the most difficult one. Here, using the data of the first three sheets, the candidate must formulate a program for himself on a daily, weekly, and monthly basis. Here is where difficult options have to be made. Most of us have enough things we want to do to fill at least a thirty-six-hour day. (I once spoke to the Lord about this but he assured me I made enough of a mess of twenty-four hours without his giving me any more to mess up.) We have to make do with what we have in time, talents, and opportunities.

Some seekers like to work out their daily schedule in timetable fashion: bed at eleven (everything begins with getting to bed in good time, something so many of us find difficult to do), up at six, exercise twenty minutes, shower, meditate twenty minutes, *lectio* ten minutes, breakfast, and so on. Others prefer to see their needs in blocks and adjust their placement according to the flow of the day: six hours sleep, two twenty-minute periods of meditation, fifteen minutes of *lectio*, and so on.

Some things need to be planned on a weekly basis. A

person who works five days a week might plan two hours of sacred study on Saturdays. A student might plan a good long physical workout on the weekend and some good space for friends. A weekly fast day is good.

A monthly day or half day of retreat is very important: taking time to look back over the month, meeting with a spiritual father, celebrating the sacrament of reconciliation, reviewing the rule of life, and enjoying some quiet time and space. Often the rule of life will need revision to respond to the onward flow of life. There is joy in realizing that our lives are moving in the direction we want instead of getting pushed around by circumstances and events.

It is obvious how useful this tool can be in the process of vocational discernment. The spiritual father can readily see where the candidate is, how much insight, clarity, and practicality he has, and help him to see this himself. Obstacles can be confronted and a practical response to them can be formulated. As the seeker returns for successive visits and the rule is reviewed, it will be evident how sincere he is, how capable he is of following a rule, how much a rule is helping him respond to life. In choosing life in a religious community or certain professions, this last point is important. Some persons will do better with a rather strict and precise rule, others will be cramped by such a rule. Each must come to discover what is best for him.

The fourth basic element in our program is learning to work with a spiritual father. The role of the vocation minister as a spiritual father is very significant in vocational discernment. We will talk about this in the next chapter.

7

Spiritual Paternity
in Vocation Ministry

I would like now to share with you some thoughts that have arisen out of personal experience since my call to serve as vocation father in my community.

First of all, I see this call as a *vocation*—a vocation within a vocation, even though it will be a fairly temporary one. It is a call from the Lord to serve him and my brothers in a specific and sometimes quite demanding but very rewarding way. It calls for a total response.

While serving in such a ministry, we must let it take priority over every other ministry if we are to have any hope of its being fruitful. That a religious community should be willing to devote some of its best men to this ministry on a full-time basis is certainly not disproportionate. In a very real sense the whole future of the community depends on the fruitfulness of this particular service. At the same time it is a very significant and much needed ministry in the Church, serving the whole Body of Christ. As vocation ministers, we should be aware of the fullness of our responsibility and the confidence that has been placed in us.

It is a vocation, a special grace and call from the Lord. The better grasp we have of this fact and what it means, the better we will serve, for we will have a better understanding of what vocation is all about.

I speak here of vocation *father* (all that I say equally applies to vocation *mother*) and not vocation *director*. There is only one director, the Holy Spirit. We need to get more in touch with our tradition, which speaks of father and mother; this more closely responds to the realities involved.

I suspect that some of us in vocation ministry might be inclined to react a bit to the concept of spiritual father. Many of us come out of an era in which there was a general reaction against the paternalism that dominated so much of Church and religious life, and unfortunately is still found in some corners. We certainly do not want to foster paternalistic attitudes. Yet we must take care to listen to today's candidates and not project on them our personal reactions and hang-ups as we seek to respond to their real needs and legitimate desires. We do not want any paternalism, but we do want to exercise and live a true spiritual, sacramental, and life-giving paternity, making present the Father's love and care.

First of all, I see the spiritual father—and I believe my understanding of this charism is formed by the tradition, a tradition still very much alive among the Christian communities of the East—as *a sacrament of God the Father*, a sacrament of his paternity and maternity. The Scriptures make it patently evident that God's care for us is tenderly maternal as well as strongly paternal. It also has the intimacy of a lover; we will speak of that later.

As spiritual fathers, supplementing, or, sad to say, often totally replacing the natural father's and mother's spiritual ministry, we are to make the Father present to the persons who turn to us. Our response is to be that of the Father: his love, his concern, his calling forth, his affirmation, his confirmation, the demands that his being and love make. To so respond, we obviously have to know the Father, and know him intimately. But *no one knows the Father but the Son and he to whom the Son will reveal him*. To fulfill our role we want to be persons who have intimate communication with the Son so that the Son can reveal the Father to us; can help us to understand the Father and the Father's response to his children. This is one of the reasons why a very important element in our lives is a daily meeting with Christ in the Gospels, listening to him, letting him speak to us about the Father. We want to listen, again and again, to those texts where Jesus speaks of the Father and his relation with him. Gradually the full import of these revealing words will sink in and form our minds and hearts, so that we begin to respond to those who turn to us in the way the Father would respond to them. It will often happen that it will be in today's prayer that we learn how to respond as the Father to the young man who comes to us today. Our Lord, using a negative expression to convey a positive reality, said: *Sufficient for the day is the evil thereof*. He gives us each day the grace, the insight we need for that day. We cannot afford to miss our daily encounter with the Lord, if we want to be prepared for the demands of the day.

In regard to this first point, we want to remember that the spiritual father's ministry is a sacramental one. He is a sacrament of the Father's presence and love. Sacraments make the reality to be present and then they are no longer needed. As spiritual fathers we want to be sensitive and perceive when it is time for us to give way. At times our ministry is a transient one in regard to a particular person. Frequently this will be true of us as vocation fathers. Our ministry often terminates rather quickly as we pass the candidate on to a novice master, or to a spiritual father more in touch with the particular direction in which the candidate discerns he should go. We want to be ready to let go and let the new spiritual father begin to fulfill this sacramental role in the life of the man. Otherwise there can arise for the candidate a confusing situation where two persons are ministering to him, superimposing one sign upon another, so that neither is clear. This particular ministry of spiritual paternity, the ministry of the vocation father, calls for a particular detachment. There needs to be careful watch that there is no subtle hanging on and no hidden or overt jealousy between a vocation father and a novice master.

A certain largeness needs to be present also in the spirit of novice masters. It will happen at times that a vocation father is called upon to fulfill the role of spiritual father for a particular candidate in the fullest sense of that role. It will be a perduring ministry and the novice master will have to respect it without jealousy. But given the ordinary sequence of development, and the freedom both ministers need in their office, this should be seen as quite exceptional.

The situation in our Western institutes is quite different from the reality as it exists among our Eastern brothers, where roles, offices, and ministries are quite simplified. In the East, a young man ordinarily goes in search of a spiritual father, and finding him, remains with him until death separates them—at least physically, for the spiritual bond often grows more intimate after death intervenes. (Perhaps I should not even say physically, for the spiritual son will often preserve with reverent care the bones of his father. I have been invited to venerate the skull of more than one spiritual father.)

Yet even when the relationship perdures, the father must take care not to stand in the way of his disciple's entering into immediate relation with the Father. He does not want to be more present as a sacrament than is truly needed.

The spiritual father is also to be *a sacrament of Christ Jesus*. Christ is Father. Saint Benedict, in his *Rule for Monasteries*, tells his monks they are to call the superior *abba* or abbot, because he holds the place of Christ in the monastery. Christ is the *Father of the world to come*. The spiritual father is to be a Christperson, one whom the Christian disciple can follow, knowing that in so doing he is following Christ. St. Paul affirmed with no uncertainty his own spiritual paternity: *You may have ten thousand peda-gogues, but only one Father. It is I who have begotten you in Christ Jesus.*

As spiritual fathers we want to have the mind of Christ: *Let this mind be in you which was in Christ Jesus.* It is not just a question of the intellect or the understanding, but of the attitude, the heart of Christ, the inner feel of Christ; in this particular instance, the feeling of Christ for each person who presents himself to us. We do want to see Christ in the candidates and respond to them as we would respond to Christ. But also we want to be Christ to them and respond to them as Christ responds to them: with love and compassion, taking on their pains, their aches, their needs, their sins.

Here let me insist again, to fulfill this role, we need to encounter Christ daily in a most intimate, listening, learning way. We want to let the Gospels speak to our hearts and form them, form this mind of Christ in us, so that we may spontaneously respond to those who come to us in the way *he* would respond. To be good Christian spiritual fathers we will spend a lot of time with the Gospels, with Christ in the Gospels. This is essential. If our ministry is not as fruitful as we would like it to be, this is the first thing we should check: Are we regularly spending *a truly significant amount of time* with Christ, letting him form our minds and hearts?

As I already began to indicate, the spiritual father must also be *a mediator*, standing before the Father with his candidates in his heart, presenting them and all their needs to the Father. When we pray, God does not listen to our lips, he looks to our hearts. We want to take those who come to us into our hearts, into our care and concern. We cannot fool them in this regard and we certainly cannot fool God. We must stand before the Father with them in our hearts, obtaining for them from the Father that gift of life which they seek—in the case of vocational ministry, the gift of a particular expression of the Christ-life among his people, the grace of a vocation.

This does mean spending time in explicit prayer for our candidates. And more importantly, it means that our candidates are in fact men we know and love and care about. They cannot be just so many cases in files. In this regard our relationship with the candidates is important, and I would like to share a few practical thoughts on this matter.

Our initial response to a candidate, an inquirer, is important. First impressions are lasting impressions. It would be sad if this response were institutional or impersonal, rather than a warm, Christlike, personal one to the full extent that the situation allows. To respond to an inquiry with a printed letter, or even a personal letter lost in a large packet or collection of printed things, is getting off on the wrong foot. The personal letter might be accompanied by a bit of printed material, but not so much as to overshadow the personal response. The personal letter can be followed by a booklet or packet, that will then arrive not as an impersonal response but as a gift from a friend. What we are concerned about is developing a loving relation in the Lord, a brotherhood in Christ, a true friendship which we hope will perdure forever, and perhaps even blossom into that special bonding that is shared religious life in community. Friendships do not usually begin with a lot of forms or written biographies. There are some men who do like to tell you all about themselves from the start. This is better done in a spontaneous letter, or better still, during a visit. I think if we are honest we will admit that forms do not really tell us that much. The factual data we need can be picked up later when it becomes clear that it is going to be needed. In most cases forms prove to be just a waste of time and paper. In using them we are, perhaps, trying to forestall spending time with someone who will obviously not have a calling to our particular community. If this is the case, are we not perhaps seeing our ministry in terms that are too narrow? If a person turns to us, writes to us, inquires of us, should it not perhaps be taken as an indication that the Lord has some role for us to play in this person's life? To be for a moment a sacrament of God's love to another person is a great privilege and can have an eternal impact. To let someone into our hearts is to begin something that will blossom in eternity, whatever its course in this life.

Letters, even in the case of the best and most open of letter writers—and most candidates do not qualify as such— offer a very limited basis for the kind of friendship in the Lord we want to develop here. Visits to the candidates in their homes can have value. But most do not have their own homes, and the prolonged, intimate sharing we want often cannot readily take place in the parental home or in shared quarters. The vocation father needs to have his own space, a place with ample accommodations so that the candidates may come when they want to and are able, and may stay for as long as they find it useful, in a space which they can identify as their place. Sensing that they have a place as a seeker within the Christian community is immensely supportive to vocation. In such a space the spiritual father and the candidate can leisurely get to know each other and explore the heart in its depths to discern what the Lord is saying. Time and space are needed for a relationship to grow. The behavioral sciences have made us aware of the importance of the supportive and proportionate environment.

As a spiritual father gets to know and love a candidate, if

the father is a man of faith in communion with the Father, mediation of the most effective sort cannot but follow.

Another dimension of our ministry of spiritual paternity is that of *example*. A father begets a son in his own image, and through education, in its strictest and most natural sense, forms him to his own likeness. If the spiritual father is fulfilling the aspects of his role which I have spoken of, he will be fulfilling what is most essential here. He will be giving an example of what is at the heart of every Christian life: an intimate relation with God in Christ, which involves that dedicated, loving listening that forms the person and his response.

All are called to intimacy with God. All are called to be lovers. God is love. We are to be like him, made in his image. As vocation fathers, in all that we say, do, and are, we want to give witness that this is the orientation of our lives. If we are to be generative of life, it will be because of a fruitfulness in Christ Jesus. Our parental love will be one with that of the Father and Jesus, because of our bond of love with them. Thus we will seek to exemplify for our candidates the kind of love-life that is to be sought. Moreover, we want to be exemplars who can teach. We want to be able to share with the candidates from our own life experience how one cultivates this love relation with the Lord. In practice we will need to develop methods which the candidate can use to begin to encounter the Lord in the Scriptures and move into quiet contemplative prayer.

When the vocation father can teach the candidate to meditate, he can help him get in touch with his deepest self and with the grace he is receiving. Essentially, vocation lies in receiving from the Lord the grace to effectively follow a particular call, the grace to be alive as a member of the whole Body in a particular way. Deep prayer helps the candidate to perceive the grace he is receiving. Deep prayer is important both for the vocation father and for the candidate. When we meditate together with our candidates, wonderful things happen.

In speaking about our role as mediators I have already spoken of friendship with the candidates, but let me speak more explicitly about this particular aspect of the spiritual father's role—that of being *friend*. If the candidates are in some respects spiritual sons, they are adult sons. An adult son is a friend. This is one of the important aspects of becoming an adult. A son must in some way break away from his parents, only to return to them to form with them a new relation, an adult relation, where he begins to take responsibility for them, a responsibility that grows with the years. As the candidates' relationship with us as spiritual father grows, the sharing will become more mutual. The candidates will grow in their own loving concern for us and will pray more for us. And they will also share more in our concerns. They will be able to enter more deeply into our vocation ministry, not only through prayer for the other candidates, but also through friendship with them, through encouragement and mutual sharing. The candidates can share our labor, whether it be the practical housekeeping and office tasks or the more spiritual ones.

Finally, the spiritual father should be a *reflective guide*. I speak of *reflective* guidance. This needs to be understood in two senses. We want to be reflective in the sense of pondering deeply in prayer, in the light of the Gospels, on all that we perceive in our contact with the candidate. Very serious and prolonged reflection in this sense is incumbent upon us. But we want also to be reflective in the sense of reflecting back to the candidate as purely and clearly as possible what we hear and see the Holy Spirit saying and doing in them. We want to be a bright and undistorted mirror for the candidate. This calls for detachment and purity of heart on our part. Our own natural feelings and reactions have to be set aside and not allowed to distort the image we send back to the candidate.

Both of these processes of reflection call for careful, open, and attentive listening. We want to provide a climate of compassionate attentiveness that will invite the candidate to seek to bring to the surface all the stirrings that are in his heart: the wonder, the fears, the longings, the passions, so that he himself can see them clearly in this mirror and evaluate them in an unpressured space and with compassionate assistance.

We are guides, not directors. We are to guide the candidate in listening and responding to the Holy Spirit, who alone has the authority to direct the human person, the son of God.

The question of obedience might be considered here. The stories from the Fathers of the Desert and the practice of some fathers among the Eastern monastics even today might raise the question of blind obedience to the spiritual father. The father is a sacrament of God the Father. *When it is clear what God wants* in a particular instance, the only adequate response is complete and unquestioning obedience. Unfortunately in most cases it is not so clear what God wants of us. Also, we must always remember that vocation is an invitation, a conditional invitation: "*If* you would be perfect. . . ." It seems to be also (though not everyone will agree with me on this) that at times and perhaps oftentimes, God in his lavish generosity invites one to several possible paths, leaving to the freedom of his beloved one the choice of which one he should choose. The greatest gift God has given to man is his freedom, the power to love, and God profoundly respects this freedom. Certainly, the spiritual father wants to fully reverence and respect the freedom of each candidate.

It is of primary importance that we as vocation fathers

know and live our own tradition and know how to teach it and hand it on to those who come to us. But we need, too, to be familiar with other traditions and practices. Many of those coming to us have had such experience. It is often an experience of this kind that first awakened a real spiritual life in them, brought them back to an abandoned Christian faith and sent them in search of a religious life. We need to be able to respond to the values they have found, give a sympathetic understanding, and help them integrate what is of value into a full Christian experience. I do not think this can be done from mere book knowledge. Besides, some experience of other practices can help us to understand, appreciate, and practice our own the better. Taking the time and effort to have such experiences will invigorate our own lives and make us more open, more truly catholic.

To be practical: It would be well to go to a local Zendo and do some sitting, or take part in a sesshin (a Zen retreat). Reading Father William Johnston or Father La Salle would be a good preparation for this, but we should do some actual sitting. For Yoga, if we cannot readily find some courses locally, or if we cringe at the thought of displaying ourselves in such postures, we could get Father Déchanet's little paperback, *Yoga in Ten Lessons*, and go ahead in the privacy of our own room. We might find the *asanas* very invigorating, and the *pranayama* might help us to control our smoking—if we have a need there. (How many candidates are turned off by a vocation father whose office is filled with unhealthy air? If you are a smoker you probably never hear this, but if you are a nonsmoker you hear it readily enough from candidates who have been around.) It is difficult for a religious to be initiated into TM (Transcendental Meditation) because of its special requirements, but one can get some idea of the TM experience by working a bit with Benson's *Relaxation Response*. TM has some similarities to Centering Prayer but there are some important and essential differences in our Christian tradition. There are also Ira Progoff's Intensive Journal Workshops and the Silva Mind Control Workshops, but few of the men I have worked with have been influenced by these.

A vocation father can certainly profit by some sensitivity experience if he has not already had something of this kind. One of the best offerings I have encountered in this area is Communications Center One in Saint Louis, run by a Maryknoll Sister and a Passionist Priest. But there are others. I already mentioned *est*, for example, in Chapter 5. The genius of Werner Erhard has put together elements from many traditions, blending them into a quite effective Western Zen experience. The *est* training involves two very strenuous weekends, but any vocation father should have it put together enough to profit a good bit from this challenge that calls forth a more vital faith.

Opening ourselves to a variety of experiences can make us more open as persons. Going through them can put us in closer touch with some of the experiences that have shaped the minds and hearts of those who come to us. Letting our own spiritual life be confronted by these vital currents can lead to a revitalization of our own prayer life. We obviously cannot practice such an assortment of exercises, but even a relatively brief experience of them will enable us to approach them from the inside when a candidate begins to share his experience with us. It seems to me it is a part of that laying down of our lives for others, for the men we are specifically called to serve as vocation fathers—this giving of our time and energy to such programs.

Important as the paternal dimension is in our vocation ministry, I think a few words of caution are in order before concluding. It is something we have already touched upon: the importance of detachment. As spiritual fathers we want always to be on the watch that in our relationship with our sons we are not in any way using them to fulfill our own needs. Every man does need to be generative. In actuality the ministry of spiritual paternity will fulfill this need in us. But nothing could frustrate the fruitfulness of our ministry as much, or do as much harm, as seeking primarily our own fulfillment and using the candidates for this end. Our ministry, our relationships with the candidates must be wholly orientated toward their well-being and growth. In doing this we ourselves will grow.

As vocation fathers we want also to be aware of the fact that we are not necessarily called to fulfill the role of spiritual paternity in regard to every seeker who comes to us. I remember well the words of a great spiritual father on Mount Athos. He said there is this difference between natural paternity and spiritual paternity: In natural paternity, it is the father who decides to become a father; in spiritual paternity, it is the son who comes and calls forth the father. Not all candidates will look to a vocation father as a spiritual father. When I first became a superior, a wise old superior wrote to me: "Remember, you cannot reach everyone." True! Not everyone will relate deeply with us as vocation fathers or call us forth as spiritual fathers. We must realize this and accept it peacefully. It is important that the candidates be open with someone as a spiritual father so that the vocation can be engendered. We should be sure that this is happening. But that someone need not necessarily be ourselves.

It is a tremendous grace to be called to serve another as spiritual father, to be to him a sacrament of the Father and of the Lord Jesus, and to be invited to share a deep, intimate, spiritual friendship. It is also a humbling grace, a very humbling one, and a painful one. For we cannot but experience how much we fail to be indeed an unsullied transparent sacrament, a fitting exemplar, an effective and faithful mediator. There is deep pain in the realization that our candidates suffer because of our limitations and infidelities. We beg the Lord insistently to make up for this. Despondency, of course, is not the proper response to these realizations. Rather, the proper response is to bear the pain redemptively with Christ, so that it will lead to our own healing and the healing of others, and to fruitfulness in the future. If we are humble enough to accept the fact that fruitfulness is not our due, but the pure gift of the superabundance of an all-loving God, then he can give us a fruitfulness beyond all our expectations.

I have touched on only a few aspects of our ministry to vocations, though I believe they are important and central aspects. There are, of course, others that are very important too. The life we mediate is the life entrusted to a community and lived out in community, and so our relation and that of the candidates with the Christian community is of the greatest importance. It is an ecclesial life, a special participation and building up of the life of the whole Body of Christ, and so relationship to the Church in her fullness is of very great importance. We want to identify our own role in Church and community and be able to help the candidate to perceive the ecclesial meaning of the role he is being invited to accept. I will say more about this later.

There are still many other aspects we can and must consider: our relations as men to the feminine in ourselves and others and vice versa; our relations to Mary, the universal mediatrix; the mystery (and it is a mystery) of truly Christian poverty, and so on. This weekend I am welcoming a candidate who has come to us by way of Buddhism, and another through TM. Such routes are the more common among our candidates today. But whatever routes they have followed, I find that all are looking for a spiritual father—for one who out of a lived experience can lead them into a fuller life in the Spirit, a fuller experience of the God of love.

A vocation, a vocation to be a father, to be a father in the spirit, evoking a recognition, calling forth and nurturing a gift of life, a participation in the life we have received in our own calling—this is how I see the ministry of a vocation father. Anything that can help us to be more fully in touch with the life we have received, and to live it more fully; anything that can help us touch more intimately, more empathetically the currents of life in the men we serve, is something we want to exploit to the full.

8

Vocational Discernment

W hen I was a young man trying to discern my vocation, I was given the impression, to put it grossly, that sometime before time, before the whole creative project got under way, the Father, Son, and Holy Spirit sat down and planned the whole thing and vocational discernment involved discovering exactly what plan they had for me. There was that one spot, that one slot for me and it was all-important for me to find it and live in it. A failure to discover it or persevere in it and all would be lost. Obviously, such an outlook did not do anything to relieve the tension involved in vocational discernment.

I do not think, however, that such an image respects the freedom of the human person nor does it respect God's great reverence for this fundamental gift which he has given to us. Nor does it do justice to his accustomed largesse. Undoubtedly, God does have particular vocations for some of his chosen ones. He did send Gabriel to Mary and Saint Bridget to Joan of Arc. The firstborn of a king does ordinarily have a vocation to be a king. The vocation, the call, is clear. At the same time, the Fathers of the Church have always extolled Mary's freedom in responding to Gabriel. Vocation is an invitation, not a command. Mary was free to say "no." It seems to me Mary would have had something less than true freedom if there was no alternative way open to her to love and serve God. The prince's vocation may seem quite clear, but I think it would still be good for him to look at other alternatives. Princes and kings have abdicated to seek what they have considered their true vocation. A response to God worthy of the human person calls for real options.

Most of us are not invited by angels or saints to serve the Lord in a special mission. Nor are we the children of kings. For most of us there are no strong, clear signs of a call to a particular vocation. And the fact of the matter is, I believe, that God does not have a "pigeon hole" for us. I believe God in his accustomed largesse gives to most of us, if not to each one of us, the gifts, graces, and abilities to do a number of things with our lives. Most men who make good monks could also have made good parish priests or missionaries, good husbands and fathers. God does not really care (if I may speak so anthropomorphically) what way we choose, so long as we do choose a way to grow in his love and choose it for love of him. I don't think we have to seek the *best* vocation for ourselves, though we might look at the different options open to us with this question in mind: which way can I best grow as a lover?

We should always and in all things seek to do God's will, to please him. To discern what that is in each case we should use proportionate means: prayer, reflection, and consultation proportionate to the matter in hand. If it is a question of how to spend an afternoon or whether to buy a book, a little prayer and reflection, perhaps a word with a friend if one be at hand, will be enough—due proportion. When it is a question of a lifetime commitment or a professional career, we may well spend some years in discernment, doing a great deal of praying and pondering while seeking the help of a spiritual father. In the end, when proportionate effort has been expended, whatever that may be, we often find ourselves with no clear answer. Then, I believe, what our Lord is actually saying to us is: I have given you your freedom. You see your possibilities. Choose whatever way you wish. We have to have the courage to choose, and then say to the Lord in substance: Lord, you haven't made it clear that you want any particular response from me, so I choose this one. I know you have the power to make it the very best and that you so love me that you will make it the very best. It is this confident love that the Lord wants. And he will confirm the vocation with his efficacious grace.

Vocation includes three graces. First of all, we see particular Christian vocations as beautiful. Every Christian vocation has a dimension of faith and, therefore, of mystery. It is living in some way the mystery of Christ. Only by grace can anyone perceive the sacramental dimension of Christian marriage. A call to celibacy for the kingdom is indeed a mystery of faith. And many of the secondary calls within these fundamental calls, such as apostolate, ministry, or religious life, can only have meaning to one whose understanding is illumined by God's grace.

For this first grace to be operative, the candidate must in some way be given the opportunity to come into contact with particular vocations so he can perceive their beauty. Religious communities can very easily set up programs and offer a hospitality which can make this possible in regard to their particular call. However, the communication of the availability of such programs to seekers seems to be more a problem. The public at large seems more aware of the openness of Hindu ashrams and Buddhist meditation centers than they are of Christian centers and monasteries. For other vocations intimate, prolonged contact is not so easily arranged. It is something those in vocation ministry and the Christian community at large should be concerned about. On first impression, we might think that the vocation to

Christian matrimony is readily available for all to consider. But I am afraid that there are few marriages where the sacramental dimension is in evidence. Most young people are exposed to an experience of marriage that does not offer an inviting insight into the beauty of Christian marriage. This is a very challenging area to which some response has been made by charismatic communities, pre-Cana conferences, and the like. Much yet remains to be done. I think this underlines how important it is that married couples and single lay Christians collaborate with the clergy and religious in the vocation ministry of the Church.

A second vocational grace we receive enables the seeker to perceive one or more of these Christian vocations as beautiful for himself. Many Christians see the monastic life as something very beautiful and this is an insight of grace. But they do not see it as beautiful for themselves. Most sense a call in other directions. Some seekers see the monastic life as a beautiful thing for themselves and at the same time see other vocations also as attractive.

Under the operation of this second grace objective criteria can come into play. A man with a tin ear or damaged vocal chords can hardly see the vocation of an opera singer as a good choice for himself no matter how much he loves the opera. A man whose attractions are exclusively homosexual will not see marriage as beautiful for himself, even though he may have a great desire to be a father and greatly appreciate home and family life. A vocation father, vocation programs, and various forms of testing can help a seeker to see more clearly the degree to which he does or does not have the objective qualities he needs for particular vocations to which he may be attracted. Sometimes the most difficult task in vocation ministry is to help a candidate to realize he does not have some of the objective qualities necessary for a particular vocation to which he is strongly attracted.

In the end, the seeker often finds himself faced with several attractive possibilities for which he has all the necessary gifts and talents. The third grace then comes into play, enabling us to choose and effectively pursue one of his options. I think it is extremely important for the candidate to take a good look at his options. It is only when we are aware of our options that we can make a fully human, and, therefore, a fully graced choice. Once the choice is made, the next step, obviously, is to begin to pursue the choice effectively. It is in this that we have the clearest evidence of the presence of a true vocation. For one cannot successfully pursue interiorly and exteriorly any Christian vocation without the grace of God. If we do succeed, not excluding the ordinary failures that mark the path of every child of Adam, we can be morally certain we are receiving the grace of the vocation, that God our Father has confirmed our choice and will continue to be with us along our chosen way.

For many, choice is difficult. Readily perceiving several beautiful possibilities for ourselves, we find it difficult to give up all that we have to give up in order to choose one. Such a choice, difficult though it be, is a good thing. Giving up very real goods for the sake of our chosen way should lead us to prize that way all the more and make us more determined to live it to the full. Sometimes it is the vocation father's task to help a candidate to see what is proportionate time, prayer, and energy to expend in discernment and then to encourage and support him in finally making a choice. It is no fun sitting on a fence, but some find it very hard to get off the fence, to let go of one or another beautiful option. When the choice is made there can be a real sense of loss. Two (or more) beautiful lives have been perceived and now the choice is made and the chooser dies to one to live to the other. In time, joy in the chosen life will heal the sense of loss. But for the moment, the candidate can use some sympathetic support and some firmness lest he climb back onto his fence.

If we see that vocation is a call expressed for most in and through the many circumstances and gifts of life, a call to a free person leaving him multiple options, much of the unneeded and unhelpful mystery is taken out of vocational discernment. It is not a question of second-guessing God but getting in touch with the goodness of God alive in ourselves. And then there is the challenging and exciting task of exploring the potential of that goodness and deciding how to exploit it. Every vocation opens out to the excitement of risk and tremendous possibilities. It is a great joy and privilege to take part in the unfolding of a life and the discovery and activation of its potential.

Undoubtedly there are some who, like myself, were taught a theory of vocation that placed all the emphasis on the antecedent will of God, and so will find emphasis on the freedom of choice in vocation a new and questionable approach. We are, indeed, here in touch with the mysterious commingling of grace and free will. For their sake let me add a couple of thoughts.

First of all, this approach to vocation is not something I have elaborated on my own. It has been put forth often enough in the last couple of decades by competent theologians. Moreover, in regards to its theological basis, it does not, in fact, differ a great deal from the more common older approach. Both approaches admit the role of the objective criteria. The older way would say that God is indicating his will through the presence or absence of these gifts. My approach, or more truly I should say our approach, sees that a candidate cannot reasonably, and, therefore, gracefully (in the strictest sense of that word), choose a vocation for which he does not have the qualifications. Hence he is not receiving the second grace of vocation; he is not called if he does not have the qualifications.

Both theories agree on the negative decisiveness of a lack of qualifications.

And both agree that the presence of qualifications is not positively decisive, for the same qualities fit one for various vocations. The older approach at this point appeals to attraction. God draws by attraction. At this point, it seems to me the older approach fails. For men are often attracted to several vocations. The older theory leaves the seeker with little guidance at this point, and often with much tension and fear. How is he to sort out the various attractions and discover which precise one is from God? Before the Second Vatican Council, vocation directors would sometimes appeal to a supposed hierarchy of vocations and proclaim that the highest attraction was obviously from God. With the clear teaching of the Holy Spirit in the Council affirming the universal call to holiness, few would think of taking such an approach today. How then is the candidate to sort out his attractions? Is it not a fact that he often has several which are good and beautiful? On what basis can we say only one is the call of God? All that is good, all that is beautiful comes from God. I think we can only conclude that God does give many, if not all of us, a multiple choice, an invitation, a call to various vocations, and stands ready to walk with us along whatever path we choose. The vocation father's task is to help the candidate to consider clearly and seriously his options, so he can make a fully human choice, and help him to make that choice inspired by motives truly worthy of him as a person loved, redeemed, and called to the intimate union of holiness.

In some ways this understanding of vocation, more consonant with the freedom of God and man, makes vocational discernment easier. But, in fact, true discernment is never easy. Options must be diligently and patiently considered in the light of faith. Our own gifts and limitations have to be objectively assessed. And in the end, what is probably most difficult, the candidate has to take full responsibility for his choice and have confidence in God's power and love.

Every vocation has its pros and cons, those things that will help the growth of love and those that will hinder. These must be weighed. In the end, the candidate would be advised to choose the one that has the most pros and the least cons, even if it be the more difficult in some respects. When he chooses he must choose the vocation with its pros and its cons. He must choose the cons also and take the responsibility for the choice and be willing to live with it. This is not easy. He must know that the pros of other vocations will challenge his choice repeatedly. When a man chooses a wife, he must choose her warts and all, and he should know well that more beautiful women (at least under some aspects) may come along. Challenged fidelity is part of the school of love. When a man lives with the realization that he is responsible for his commitment, that he cannot blame God for forcing him into such a way, I think he is in a much healthier position to grow in his chosen way of love. The role of the vocation father to challenge a candidate and help him take conscious responsibility for his life is sometimes a very difficult one, but always a privileged and gracefilled one. The opportunity to respond freely to God with the gift of our lives is one of the most precious things he has given to each one of us.

9

The Vocation of the Church
The Role of the Church
in the World

When we speak of Christian vocation it is always and necessarily within a community, among a pilgrim people, in the Church. As a community, a Church, we have a vocation which provides a context for our particular vocations, enlivens them, and expands their horizons. Before completing our considerations on Christian vocation, I would like to share a few thoughts on the vocation of the Church, our Church, Christ's Church, the Church which we are, in the world today.

Let us begin with a simple and basic affirmation—one that we all share. Jesus Christ is our Master. He is our Lord, our Life, our Love. We are his people, the Christian people, because he is our Master. We follow him and look to him for the truth, for he is Truth.

Jesus used many images to speak of us, his Church: the leaven that is to leaven the whole; a tiny mustard seed that is to become a great tree, sheltering all; a net with a mixed catch; a field that would yield its good crop, yet with an admixture of weeds even until the harvest.

Jesus commissioned us his Church to go forth and teach. We are to be bearers of his truth—more importantly, bearers of him who is Truth. Because we have him, we have all truth. We have all the answers—and yet we do not have all the answers. Implicitly, in him and his guiding Spirit we do have all the answers. Explicitly, in our own consciousness, we are a learning Church. Together in Council we have said:

> The tradition which comes from the Apostles develops in the Church with the help of the Holy Spirit. For there is a growth in the understanding of the realities and the words which have been handed down. This happens through the contemplation and study made by believers, who treasure these things in their hearts, through the intimate understanding of spiritual things they experience, and through the preaching of those who have received through episcopal succession, the sure gift of truth. For, as the centuries succeed one another, the Church constantly moves forward toward the fullness of divine truth until the words of God reach their complete fulfillment in her. (Constitution on Divine Revelation, *Dei Verbum*, n. 8.)

We are learners, yet teachers as well. Herein lies at times a painful tension. To illustrate, let us revert to one example that rests deep in our hearts at this time: the question of the call of women to the ministerial priesthood. We are a learning Church. We listen to the signs of the times, to the evolution in human consciousness of the dignity of persons, to the development of social and ecclesial relationships, needs, and responsibilities, to the movement of the Spirit within our own spirit; and then we give dignified witness to what we hear. We are a learning Church, and spur on our theologians and scripture scholars to reflect more deeply on the data of the Revelation in the light of what we are hearing. With them, we spur on our duly constituted teachers, those who sit today, not on the chair of Moses, but on the chair of our Master, the Lord Jesus, and his Apostles, that they might hear what we are learning, and under the Spirit proclaim what the Spirit is saying to the Churches today.

And it is "Churches." We are humbly conscious that we are Church, and so are our brothers and sisters in Africa, Asia, South America, Europe, and Australia. All must be listened to; the witness of each must be reflected upon. With such an immense body of faithful, the process is slow. We live with tensions.

As a Catholic brother I am very proud of our sisters who have taken such responsible leadership in the promotion and proclamation of the equality and dignity of women, and the dignified and faith-filled way in which they have abided in the tensions of a learning and teaching Church.

The Church must teach, it must teach prophetically in the Spirit and never give way to the pressure of popular sentiment or demand. But to fulfill our role as a teaching Church, we must first be a listening Church.

Above all, and before all, we must listen to Christ, our Master. Anyone who claims to be a Christian but is not thoroughly and intimately formed by the words of the Holy Gospel, is deceiving himself or herself and others. We must then turn to the Gospels each day. Daily Gospel listening is a fundamental duty of every Christian.

We must listen to our brothers and sisters in the community of the faithful, to those of the past and those of the present, to their faith-filled reflections and lived experience. We are a community, a body, that transcends space and time, and it is together we hear the Word of the Lord, the Good News we are to live and proclaim as the Way to fuller life and to all happiness.

We must also listen to creation, to nature. Through

centuries, with great care, the Church elaborated a stable concept of the law of nature to guide us in our response to, use of, and collaboration with the Creative Word of God expressing himself in the creation. Yet the time has surely come to question the validity of a static concept of created nature and its exigencies. We, the Church, must search for a dynamic natural law which is consonant with a rapidly evolving creation. Whether the practical conclusions that will flow from such a dynamic concept of natural law will be the same as those that now guide us, we cannot say a priori. But if the Church is to fulfill faithfully her teaching role for our times and what lies ahead, we must have the courage to explore the significance of all the signs of the times.

With sensitivity and compassion we must challenge our stewardship of the creation. A true ecology, I believe, can emerge only from a heightened awareness of our oneness not only with all persons but with all created things which at every moment, one with each one of us, come forth from the creative love of our common Father. We cannot remain theoretical here, but as Church we must be practical and give practical witness.

By way of example: If all the grain that is used to produce the high-content alcoholic beverages that we Americans consume were preserved as grain and served to the hungry, there would be no hunger on our planet. And if the funds that we Americans spend on these beverages went into a fund for feeding, the grain could easily be distributed. What does such a fact dictate in regard to our own use of alcohol and that of the immediate ecclesial community to which we belong and in which we have a shared responsibility?

Again, if the land used to raise tobacco were converted to food-producing crops and the funds spent on tobacco directed to getting the produce of these lands to the needy, there would be no famine on the earth. What, then, must the Christian and the Christian community proclaim in practice in regard to the use of tobacco?

Pope John Paul II has reminded us recently that we must give even of our substance, but here we speak of what are in fact harmful superfluities!

We could go on in this vein and touch upon many vital areas of economic, political, and technological life, listening to what the dignity of the human person, the image of God, with his unalienable right to life, liberty, and the pursuit of happiness, postulates in teaching, in living, in witnessing and proclaiming the Good News.

We as a particular Christian Church need to listen to the other Christian communities. Already in our times they have effectively recalled us to a fuller appreciation of the Scriptures, of the charismatic dimension of Christian life, of the ministry of healing, of the power and need of joyful Christian community. We need yet to hear more from our Orthodox brothers and sisters about transcendence in worship, the power of symbols, the perduring value of tradition. Our Quaker brethren call us to the attentiveness of silent listening in personal and communal prayer; the Shakers, to the joy of Christian dance. The Latter Day Saints and Jehovah's Witnesses challenge us with their missionary zeal and point out how we have failed to call forth our young adults, the most alienated segment of our Church.

By hearing our brothers and sisters and responding to these values in our own heritage we affirm our fellow Christians even as we grow ourselves. And we in turn must recall them to that value which our Master made the heartfelt concern of his priestly prayer—the unity of his followers and the need of an authority to authenticate the validity of our lived experience and personal and communal discernment.

But our listening must go beyond Christian communities

and even beyond our Jewish forebears and our Moslem cousins to the ancient religions of the East. Their masters invite us to rediscover our own mystical tradition, what it means to be disciples of a Master, and the importance of the role of the spiritual mother and father—a figure strikingly present whenever Christian spirituality has been most vital, but which is hardly visible in our day. And we can bring our witness to our Eastern brethren, enriching their experience of universal compassion with the reality of the Mystical Body, transforming the yogic asanas into integral acts of worship which fully link the body and soul in homage, and elevating the watched breath of meditation to a sacramental breathing-in of the Spirit, and breathing him forth with the Son in creative healing love for the universe in communion with the Father.

The Church is to be present in openness and respect, to listen, to assimilate, to transform and elevate, and to proclaim a call to a transcendent fullness in Christ.

We must listen to every people and to every nation, to the cultures within the nations and beyond the nations, to the black, the white, the yellow, and the red, to each minority, no matter how disenfranchised; to the generations, the young, the old, and the mid-lifers; to the classes—upper and lower, blue collar and middle; to the social systems—communist and capitalist, socialist and tribal, knowing that each has its vision of the truth and in some way seeks the truth in justice, and in that reveals a facet of Christ, the Truth, and challenges us as Church to respond to and affirm that reality and to consciously promote its realization in our midst. All things are ours, and we are Christ's, and Christ is God's.

Never before in the history of the human race has a people or a nation stockpiled weapons and in the end not used them. In our times nations have stockpiled weapons in unprecedented numbers and power. Their use would mark the end of a civilization, if not of the race and the planet. Our only hope is that we can break with the patterns of the past, and rising to a new level of consciousness, forgo the use of our weapons, turn swords into ploughshares, and feed the family. Many of our Eastern brethren, through their disciplines, now widely taught in our own country and within our own Christian communities, seek an enlightenment that issues in a universal compassion. Our own Christian tradition summons us to a contemplative experience where we touch the ground of our being and know that, one with all, we emerge constantly from the creative love of God, sharers in his being and life. From this experience flows a connatural reverence for all life and even the "inanimate," and a clear sense that any harm we do to another we do to ourselves and to all whom we love, and that any misuse of the created is sacrilege. When such realization and insight colors all our thinking and doing, we have attained a new level of consciousness. We live under the impulse of the Holy Spirit and his gifts. Teilhard de Chardin spoke of this as the noosphere and saw all centered in and moving toward an Omega point which he properly identified as the Heart of Christ, the great sacrament of God's love, which he made one with his very self in the Incarnation.

The Church, by rediscovering, effectively teaching, and living its contemplative dimension, and by affirming and collaborating with the thrust of every other spiritual tradition and discipline that seeks the evolution of human consciousness to this new and higher level centered in love, preeminently fulfills her mission in the world today and gives us hope that there will be a world tomorrow to continue to glorify the Father in the Son through the Holy Spirit.

There is another aspect of the Church's mission in the world which we cannot pass over in silence. We hear of it in

Saint Paul's mysterious words: we are to fill up what is wanting in the Passion of Christ. By our participation we are to make his saving mission actual today. We hear more today of the Church being persecuted—in some places violently, in some places subtly. It should not surprise us but assure us. *Blessed are you when you suffer persecution for my name's sake.* The Lord's word: *Unless the grain of wheat fall into the ground and die, it remains itself alone* does not apply to us only as individuals, but also as ecclesial communities. We are called to share the cross in our own lives and in the lives of others. It is because we live so far from our own center, from the ground of our being, that we, in the affluent countries, are able to share in an inhumanly exploitive affluence that demands such a price from our brothers and sisters in other lands and even in the ghettoes of our own. We, as individuals and as Church, need to enter into the redemptive pain of true compassion, and a reshaping of our conduct will follow.

If our motivating understanding of the mission of the Church is anything less than union and communion with every person on the earth and beyond, a union with the whole fabric of the creation in an uplifting that is a participation in Christ's Ascension, we have betrayed our challenging and truly transcendent evangelical vocation.

10

A Closing Word

In the opening days of the UN's Second General Conference on Disarmament, in June 1982, I had the privilege, the grace, and the joy to be part of a powerful witness for peace. Over a million men and women of all ages and many nations came together in New York's Central Park, to say peacefully but powerfully, "We want peace, and we want it now." The leaders of the nations and the leaders of the multinationals have ears and they hear not. We must continue to speak peacefully and powerfully for peace.

Early on the day of the witness we gathered in our assigned places under our proper banners. I walked with the Benedictines for Peace. As we advanced from the United Nations toward Central Park, other groups merged into the stream and intermingled. At one time I found myself among white-turbaned Sikhs, at another under the banner of a Gay Liberation contingent, then I was with the Marxist-Leninists, and later with Caesar Chavez's United Farm Workers. When we reached Central Park, all the banners came down. We were one people, the human family, with one concern: peace on earth, a common goodwill among us.

Each of us does have his or her proper vocation, our proper identity among a pilgrim people. It is important that each one of us does discern, choose, and live out, according to our proper gifts and talents, a particular vocation among God's people. We each have a unique contribution to make, one that no one else can ever make. Some of us, perhaps many of us, do not readily accept this. We do not see our lives as that significant. We tend rather to see ourselves as just ordinary people, lost in the crowd: another married couple, another minister or religious, carrying out daily tasks that others could just as easily do.

Inevitably it seems to me that such an understanding of ourselves and our lives must be producing in us a certain frustration. At times, I know, we have been encouraged to accept such an understanding of our lives as the humble thing to do. But true humility resides in truth and is consonant with who we really are and our true aspirations. The most humble of women, a young girl from a "hicktown"— can anything good come out of Nazareth?—dared to sing: *All generations will call me blessed for he who is mighty has done great things for me.* There is deep within each one of us a desire, a call to greatness. Humility recognizes this, and recognizes its Source, who is also the Source of its fulfillment.

Each of us does have his or her absolutely unique contribution to make to the ultimate fullness and beauty of the creation. True, he who can raise up sons of Abraham out of the very stones can raise up someone to accomplish any task we might be doing, great or small. But in the end there is one thing that only we can bring to the creation, that no one else can ever bring, and without which the whole creation project will in some way be incomplete—and that one thing is *our personal love.* No one else can ever give God, our fellow human beings, or the rest of creation our personal love. If we do not bring this gift to God and others, they will never receive it. Herein lies our uniqueness and the uniqueness of all we do. For ultimately all that anyone does has value only insofar as it is an expression of love. God is love and only the loving act expresses his creative power and presence. It is precisely this power and presence made present by our love that makes even our apparently insignificant lives and doings infinitely significant, powerful, and creative.

It is said *the just lives by faith*. It is by faith we perceive the splendid transcendent meaning in our lives and truly live. A vocation is Christian when it is informed by faith and love of Christ, when it is a following of him who saved the world and gave infinite glory to the Father as a growing child, a student, a carpenter's apprentice, a teacher and minister, a friend and a leader, a political prisoner, and an executed criminal, because he sought always to do the things that please the Father. It does not really matter what we do, what role we play in this world; if we are acting out of true love—we cannot separate love of God and love of our fellows, nor can we separate love and seeking to do the things that please the Father—what we are doing has all the power and significance of the creative love of God and the redemptive love of Christ.

Therefore, none of us should underestimate the importance of his or her own vocation, even if it is one that we have been left free to choose for ourselves. It is important to choose and then live that choice to the full as a school of love, a way of love. The important role of the vocation minister is to help each to discern and choose wisely in the light of this call to empowering and all-fulfilling love. The Church in the proclamation of the Good News must exercise a very clear and practical vocational ministry. The transcendent understanding of our Christian call may seem to be very solid meat. In the ministry it must be transformed to the extent necessary to be presented as an easily absorbed, nourishing milk available to all Christ's little ones. No Christian should be left in ignorance of the sub-

limity of his or her vocation, of his or her unique importance and greatness, of his or her significance to each one
of us. The "ordinary, everyday" Christian factory worker
or housewife, clerk or entrepreneur, should personally
hear this Good News and know that he has a uniquely
important and beautiful vocation.

With our identity clear and secure we can then merge
into the flow of mankind toward its goal and make our
unique and essential contribution. Our particular vocation
and our response to it is not something apart from the
universal call of the Church and the human family through
time and space. From the day he called forth Adam until
the recapitulation of all in Christ, God is calling. Our
particular response brings us into that great concourse. We
do not lose our identity, we do not fail to make our unique
contribution, but we are part of the whole, a whole that will
not be complete without us. We walk arm in arm, monks
and nuns, Sufis and Marxists, gays and farm workers, all of
us, vitally conscious that we as Christians have something
unique and uniquely important to bring to the march of
life, the gathering of the human family into the realm of
perfect peace.

The fostering of Christian vocations should not be the
concern only of those in vocation ministry. Anyone who
loves the Body of Christ and Christ the Head, with his
universal salvific mission, will share a deep concern that all
the functions of the Body, for its own sake and the sake of
the whole human family, will be fulfilled. We tend to have
a heightened sense of the need of certain vocations and a
more acute experience of loss when there are not a sufficient number of Christians responding to them. This is
understandable. But an enlivened faith will be increasingly
aware of the importance of a generous response to every
Christian vocation for the overall health and vitality of the
Body and its redemptive mission in the world.

This awareness will call us to earnest prayer for all Christian vocations. We have a solid basis for our prayer. He has said: *Ask and you shall receive.* He listens to us; he listens more to our hearts than to our words. Our heartfelt concern, coming from a lively faith, will be before him, pleading more eloquently than Solomon in the Temple, pleading with all the power of a Christ on the Cross, our Mediator. In this most important respect vocation ministry, ministering to vocations, pertains to all Christians.

This same awareness will also express itself in the way parents will call forth their children, educate them, and support them in vocational choice. *Faith comes through hearing.* Through hearing in word and deed the faith of their parents, children will come to that level of faith awareness that they will have the grace and the joy of discerning and pursuing a particular vocation as a Christian vocation. The same role falls proportionately to pastors, to educators, to relatives, to friends, to all fellow travelers among the pilgrim people of Christ. A thoughtful question, a shared joy, a lived example, along with our concerned prayer, effectively express our love, our care, our support, and our hope, and help our brothers and sisters, younger and older, to find their Christian vocation and fulfill their role in the Body of Christ to our own enrichment and that of the entire human family. So tightly interwoven are the human family and the members of Christ that every person's vocation is the concern of us all and a gift to us all. We cannot afford to retain any narrow or specialized idea of vocation. We all have the privilege of being called and the privileged duty of supporting each other in response to a call—a call to Infinite Love.

SEABURY BOOKS OF RELATED INTEREST:

Donald Nicholl
Holiness

J. L. G. Balado
The Story of Taize (Illustrated)

Brother Roger
Living Today for God

Brother Roger
A Life We Never Dared Hope For

Brother Roger
Parable of Community:
The Rule and Other Basic Texts of Taize

Gene Ruyle
Making a Life:
Career, Commitment and the Life Process

Kevin T. Kelly
Divorce and Second Marriage:
Facing the Challenge

M. Basil Pennington
Monastic Journey to India

Deane William Ferm
Alternative Life-Styles Confront the Church